Note
Whilst every effort has been made to ensure that the content of this book
is as technically accurate and as sound as possible, neither the author nor the
publishers can accept responsibility for any injury or loss sustained as a result
of the use of this material.

Published by A&C Black Publishers Ltd
36 Soho Square, London W1D 3QY
www.acblack.com

Copyright © 2010 Iain Macintosh

ISBN 978 1 4081 1497 1

A CIP catalogue record for this book is available from the British Library.

Acknowledgements
Cover photograph © shutterstock.com
Illustrations by kja-artists.com
Designed by James Watson

This book is produced using paper that is made from wood grown in managed,
sustainable forests. It is natural, renewable and recyclable. The logging and
manufacturing processes conform to the environmental regulations of the
country of origin.

Typeset in Giovanni Book by seagulls.net

Printed and bound in Berkshire, England by Cox & Wyman

Contents

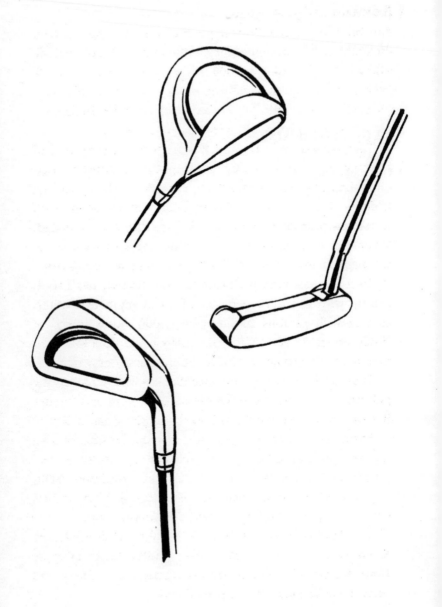

Acknowledgements

This book is dedicated to the good people at Zone Content, the finest digital content agency in the world, who offered me a desk in their building in 2009, asking nothing in return aside from a gentle request that I stop putting Bernard Cribbins on the communal Spotify. James Freedman, Anna Kissin and Jon Davie's generosity will not be forgotten in a hurry.

Thanks specifically to the staff at Icons.com, a subsidiary of Zone Content, who actually had to put up with me in their office. Dan Jamieson, Tom Rollett, Steve Ryan, Alison Ratcliffe and Jake Taylor are all very patient, understanding people who now know more about golf than perhaps they ever wanted to. If you ever want authentic sports merchandise from some of the biggest names in football, I suggest you pay them a visit.

Over the past year, my beautiful wife Rachael has had to put up with about 70 per cent of all of my conversations starting with gambits like 'I wrote 2,000 words today,' or '5,000 down, 25,000 to go!' She really could do a lot better than me but, bless her, she never points it out to my face.

Thanks must go to the creative visionary that is my publisher Charlotte Atyeo, whose idea this was, and to Lucy Beevor, who kicked the drafts into shape with great valour.

Shrimperzone, Southend's most popular fan-site, was an invaluable source of aid. Thanks go out to Napster, Steveo, Johnny Stokes, Canvey Shrimper, Uxbridge Shrimper, Stats, Boywonder2, DaveWebbsBrain, East Stand Blue, Pubey, Cricko, West Road Shrimper, LondonFatso and ORM.

Thanks also to Tony Pearson, Toby Fuhrman, Tom Warren, Shaun Nickless, Dan Bourke, James Findlay, Matt Gallagher, Dave Adams, Phil Adams, Mikey Grady, Amy Grady and everyone at The Junction in Tufnell Park.

Author's note

The idea of this book was to kick the door in on a seemingly impenetrable mass of rules and conventions, allowing the reader to comprehend the incomprehensible. Golf is a bewildering sport for the uninitiated and my primary objective was to make it all nice and simple. Because of this, I've constantly referred to golfers in the masculine. I know that in these enlightened times I probably shouldn't, but I just felt that the book would be more accessible if it didn't contain lines like 'at which point, he or she would pick up the ball and place it down next to his or her club.'

I'm not sexist, I certainly don't believe that golf is the exclusive province of men, I just like to try and write things that people can read without getting nosebleeds. Let's hope it's worked.

Iain Macintosh

Why you should like golf

Of all the sports in existence, golf must have the worst reputation by a country mile. Ask a complete stranger to name the first thing that comes into their head when they think about it and I guarantee you that they'll say 'silly trousers'. Never mind the fact that the vast majority of golfers play in the most conservative of slacks, it's always the silly trousers that stick in the mind.

Ask someone else and they might tell you that it's boring. Or that it's a game for rich people. Ask a particularly smug friend and they'll probably repeat Mark Twain's alleged observation that 'golf is a good walk spoiled,' or Winston Churchill's sage analysis that 'golf is a game whose aim is to hit a small ball into an even smaller hole with weapons singularly ill-designed for the purpose'. Wise words indeed, although I do wonder if anyone ever asked him quite how he expected to fit a small ball in an even smaller hole…

Yet for all of this negativity, golf continues to be one of the most universally popular sports in the world. Huge attendances are recorded at the major events, millions of people play it every day and the TV audiences can be staggeringly large. So it's obviously not that boring…

The truth is that golf can be utterly fascinating. It is one of the few games where the majority of the work takes place between the ears of the protagonists. For all the immense skill and training that it takes to become a professional golfer, nerves of steel are the most vital component of any champion's arsenal. Everything in the game always seems to come down to the ability of a player to do something that should be very simple. Hit a ball hard. Hit it on to the green. Get it near the hole. Tap it into the hole. Unlike other sports, no one tries to tackle you and no one tries to hurt you. Unless you're a British player in America, it's very rare that spectators will even shout anything at you to put you off. And yet it still goes wrong so often.

There are tactics and techniques, difficult choices and easy options. Play percentages and stay safe over the 18 holes of tense competition or live by the sword and experiment with a risky long shot? Hit it over the trees and save yourself a stroke? What if you don't clear the trees?

Watch a competition on the television and you'll see the full range of human emotions passing in front of you. There's the despair of a player who misses an easy putt and slips out of the reckoning. The steely-eyed glare of a competitor who has excelled at the last three holes, soared into contention and doesn't want to do anything to hex his luck. The ever-changing swirl of the leaderboard as the runners and riders swap places on the final day. And yet it all comes down to the ability of a player to hit a small ball with a large stick.

This book will not teach you how to hold a club or how to put the perfect amount of topspin on a shot. Believe me, you don't want my advice on anything like that. It once took me 11 swings to progress 100 yards up the fairway and I'm still renowned in some quarters for managing to lose a ball in Urban Golf, the hi-tech simulator where players stand in a closed cubicle and hit balls through laser sensors into a sheet of netting. The staff there told me that no one else had ever done that before. The funny thing about golf, however, is that your interest in the sport is never adversely affected by your own incompetence. Golfers simply continue to ride out the storm of shanks and slices, resolute and brave, convinced that one day everything will be alright.

No, this book certainly won't help your swing, but it will tell you how golf works and why it's so fascinating. It will explain precisely what golfers are trying to do and how they're trying to do it. With no jargon and precious few technical terms passing without explanation, you'll find within these pages everything that you could need to know to enjoy the sport. It's not an exhaustive and comprehensive examination of absolutely every aspect of the game, because there simply isn't room; it's just an introduction to a wider world. By the end of this book you'll know the difference between a birdie and a bogey, how to play 'skins' and how to calculate your handicap. You'll find out how the professional tours work, what the Majors are and perhaps even who the greatest golfer of all time was.

Golf is one of the few sports that you can play competitively even after you pick up your free bus pass. In fact, while this book was being written, a 59-year-old nearly won The Open, the equivalent of Kevin Keegan being recalled to the England 2010 World Cup squad. Thanks to the handicap system, it's possible for a professional and a relative novice to play a round together at the same time. Even I scored a bogey on a golf course once, and there must have been professionals who have done worse on that hole at some point in their lives.

It hasn't always been the case, but golf is now as inclusive and accessible as it has ever been, which is rather good timing on your part. However, if you're ever going to slip on your spiky shoes and head out to the fairway, or even if you just want to sit in front of the television and plug yourself into The Open, then you're going to need to know how it all works.

Step this way, my friend. I'll be your caddy for this round.

The history of golf

Mankind has striven since the dawn of time to achieve certain goals: to settle, to procreate, to prosper and to hit things with sticks. In the last of these base objectives we find the origins of golf, one of the oldest sports in human history. As you can imagine with an activity thought to have emerged at some point in the 13th century, details of those early days are sketchy at best.

There is evidence dating all the way back to medieval times of popular stick and ball games in continental Europe, but the most likely ancestor to the sport we know now was 'chole', a Belgian pastime where iron-headed clubs were used to thwack a wooden ball towards a target in a set number of attempts. This was introduced to Scotland in 1421, apparently by a Scottish regiment who had been off assisting the French in a battle against the English. The Scots took 'chole' and made a few subtle changes to improve it, most importantly by adding a hole for the ball to be aimed at. Golf was born, but it wasn't a simple infancy.

In 1457, with contemporary wars being won and lost by the skill and accuracy of longbowmen, King James II banned the new sport on the basis that it was stopping people from practising their archery. The ban, which was widely ignored anyway, was overturned in 1502 and the game was given the royal seal of approval when James IV became the first man in history to splash his wages on golf clubs, placing an order with a canny bowmaker from Perth who obviously knew a gap in the market when he saw one.

Royal endorsement really got things moving. Mary, Queen of Scots was one of the first leading ladies of golf, although her quest for a scratch handicap came to an end in 1587 when her cousin ordered her execution. In England, 60 years later, Charles I was a keen enthusiast and was actually halfway through a round when he heard that the Irish Rebellion had begun. Showing early signs of the natural judgement that would eventually truncate his career as king, he opted to stay out on the fairways and finish the game. He too would lose his head before he could challenge for a Major.

At some point in the 15th century, Scottish golfers began to mark out holes on a strip of land by the sea near Fife, the link between the land and the sea in fact, hence the reason why coastal golf courses are often called 'links'. There were 11 in total that stretched away from the St Andrews clubhouse and they were played in order out to the furthest one and then reversed and played back in the other way. In 1764, the owners, the Royal and Ancient Golf Club, decided that the first four holes were too short, so they were combined into two larger ones. Nine out and nine in. Now, instead of playing 22 holes in a round, golfers would play 18, a number that would be standardised and then form the basis for the modern game.

In 1744, the Gentlemen Golfers of Leith created a first draft of rules for the sport, a wonderful document which contains gems like 'if a ball be stopp'd by any person, horse or dog, or anything else, the ball so stopp'd must be played where it lyes' and 'your tee must be on the ground'. Quite where they were putting the tees before that rule was brought in is anyone's guess.

Up until the early 17th century, golf was played with wooden balls, but the invention of the 'featherie' ball changed all of that. Now balls were constructed from leather pouches filled with boiled goose feathers and covered with paint. These new balls were expensive, cursed with an irregular flight path and had a nasty habit of exploding in wet weather when they impacted on hard surfaces, but, my word, they went further than the wooden ones.

In 1848, they were superseded by the 'guttie', or gutta-percha ball. This was far cheaper to construct and, because it was made from the rubbery sap of the Sapodilla tree, it could be heated and moulded into a perfect sphere. Manufacturers quickly discovered that the balls with imperfections on the surface flew truer and further, and so the modern golf ball's ancestor came into existence.

In 1860, a golf tournament by the name of The Open was played at Prestwick Golf Club, Scotland. Only eight professionals competed in the first year, but the organisers' decision to invite amateur players the following year saw a significant increase in competitors. The Open would go on to be recognised as the world's first Major golf tournament, providing an excuse for supercilious know-it-alls to publicly humiliate anyone foolish enough to refer to it as 'The British Open' in polite company. If you learn nothing else from this book, keep this in mind. The Open is The Open. Not the British Open, not the UK Open, just The Open.

The early years of the 20th century saw a number of major changes to the sport, changes that enabled golfers to hit the ball further and more accurately than ever before. The rubber-cored ball flew far further than its predecessor, especially when it was covered with the recognisable dimples of today's version. The wooden-shafted clubs were replaced by steel and their faces, the bit that you hit the ball with, were changed from a flat to a grooved surface. All of this was achieved at lower cost and manufactured at a faster rate, making golf a more accessible sport for the masses.

Not that it was accessible to all of the masses. The Professional Golfers' Association of America (PGA), formed in 1916, didn't get around to striking a 'Caucasians Only' clause from their constitution until 1961, and for decades the only black faces to be seen on a golf course were the caddies, charged with carrying the players' bags. If the PGA believed that black men couldn't play as well as their white counterparts, emphatic evidence to the contrary would arrive in 1997.

In 1927, with two powerbases of golf building up on either side of the Atlantic, the Ryder Cup was conceived, a team event where the USA took on a combination of British and Irish players. A series of matches would be played between individual players, and also foursomes, from both teams, with points being awarded for victories and draws. The tournament, spread over a number of days, would be hotly contested until the post-war period, when the Americans got really, really good and it ceased to be much fun for either side. In 1979, the British finally decided to invite other Europeans into their ranks, a decision in no way influenced by the emergence of the legendary Seve Ballesteros, a uniquely gifted golfer from Spain.

The year 1933 saw the completion of the famous Augusta golf course which would be the home of the US Masters from 1934. The course, perhaps the most beautiful in the world, was co-designed by the supremely talented American golfer Bobby Jones. Jones wasn't just a phenomenal talent, he also epitomised the spirit in which the game was supposed to be played. In the 1925 US Open, he accidentally nudged the ball as he prepared to swing. No one noticed, but Jones immediately reported the foul to the course marshals. The two-stroke penalty cost him the championship, but Jones refused to take any credit for his honesty. 'You may as well praise a man for not robbing a bank,' he said.

The growth of golf was curtailed in the war years as global supplies of rubber and steel became scarce. One Major after another was discontinued and the US manufacture of golf equipment was halted entirely as priorities changed dramatically. When the war eventually ended, production kicked back in again and golf, with the aid of television coverage, became more popular than ever before.

The 1960s was arguably the golden age of the sport. Three exceptional players came to the fore. Arnold Palmer, Jack Nicklaus and Gary Player scrapped for supremacy across the world, with Palmer winning six Majors in the decade, Nicklaus going one better with seven and Player pitching in with four. Nicklaus would end the decade with one of the most sporting gestures in the history of the game, when he conceded a crucial Ryder Cup hole, preferring to draw the tournament rather than insist on Tony Jacklin going through the trauma of making a two-foot putt to save his team. 'I don't think you ever would have missed that putt,' he told Jacklin, 'but under the circumstances, I would never give you the opportunity.'

The most famous golf shot of all time was made in 1971 when astronaut Alan Shephard took a 6 Iron with him on a trip to the moon. Using an improvised one-handed technique to avoid damaging his spacesuit, Shephard took just one small swing for a man, but one giant swing for mankind. Incidentally, it's well worth looking up the footage of this on the Internet just to read the comment by one outraged viewer demanding to know why there was no sound. In space, no one can hear you swing.

Golf changed forever in 1997 when a young black man by the name of Eldrick 'Tiger' Woods blew the field away in the US Masters. Woods took the championship by a record margin of 12 strokes, leaving some of the biggest names in the sport trailing in his wake. In what had once been the exclusive domain of the rich white man, an African-American reigned supreme. A huge swathe of people who had never even considered playing the game suddenly had a champion. His genius was confirmed in 2001 when he completed what has come to be known as the 'Tiger Slam'. Wins in the US Open, The Open and the PGA Championship in 2000 were capped with a victory in the first Major of the 2001 season, the US Masters. For a brief period of time, Woods held every Major prize.

Golf has continued to grow in popularity in the 21st century, attracting a more diverse range of players than ever before. With the advent of Internet trading, it's easier than ever to pick up a cheap set of second-hand clubs, and there are very few days in the calendar when you can't find some live golf on the television. It's been almost six hundred years in the making, but you've finally discovered it. Welcome to the game of golf.

The basics

In a nutshell

Golf is actually a very straightforward sport. There is only one objective and it couldn't be any easier to comprehend. From a fixed starting position, you must hit a small ball with a big club as many times as it takes before it goes down a hole somewhere in the distance. The fewer times you hit it, the better you are doing. Simple, isn't it? If only.

Hitting a golf ball down a hole is far easier said than done. For starters, you have to do it 18 times to complete a round, a feat which requires huge reserves of concentration and patience. Each of those 18 stages is known as 'a hole' and some holes are nastier than others. Every golf course in the world will have a mixture of short and long holes, some with sand bunkers, some with water obstacles, some with great big bends in and some that are designed specifically to trap a vicious crosswind that will play havoc with the flight of the ball. Course designers, you'll discover, are horrible individuals who were not given enough affection as children.

But the course is only half the problem. Every golfer has a bag of clubs which come in a variety of shapes and sizes and they all have different capabilities. Some are used to power the ball vast distances, some are better for medium distances and others are used to chip the ball out of rough grass or sand. Golfers must be able to decide which club to use and at what time because the wrong decision can be incredibly costly.

A golfer is expected to count up the number of times he hits the ball, known as 'strokes', and add them up at the end of the 18 holes to calculate a final score. There are many ways to play golf, as you'll find out in the next few chapters, but the most common is 'stroke play'. This means that a simple comparison of scores is used to judge the winner. If you take 80 shots to complete your round and your opponent takes 82, then you are the winner by two strokes. In a competition, large numbers of golfers will play the same course, with the lowest score denoting the eventual winner.

But before we get down to all of that, let's have a closer look at the key areas of the game.

Getting around
The course

So, you pull up in the car park, haul your bag of clubs out of the boot and there it is stretched out in front of you like a garish 1970s carpet, all bright green and vivid splashes of yellow. The golf course. Your nemesis. You're here to play a hypothetical game of strokeplay against a hypothetical opponent by the name of Nigel Parker. You know your mission, you know that you are here to hit a golf ball down a hole, but, my word, doesn't it look terrifying when you're up close and personal? 18 holes of nastiness just waiting to catch you out. The course is almost always played in order, from 1 through to 18, so let's have a look at the opening holes.

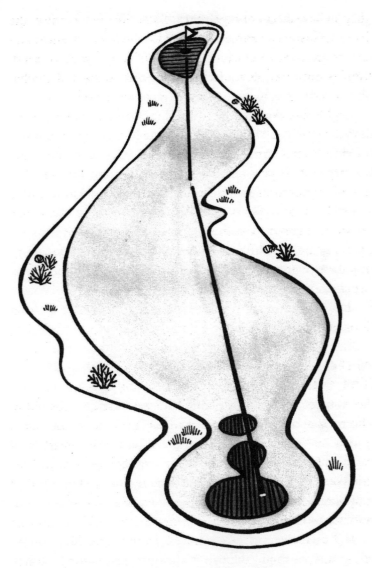

A generic par 4 hole without
a bunker or water hazard

Every hole begins with a shot from the tee. You'll recognise a tee quite easily: it looks like a very small plastic egg cup on a spike and every golfer should have a handful of them in their bag. The spike is pushed into the ground and the ball placed on top in the cup, suspending it an inch or so above the ground. Most golfers 'tee off' with a big club called a driver, and having a raised ball makes it far easier to hit with the middle of the clubface. Teeing off is the only time that a golfer can hit the ball in this manner, so it's important to make the most of it.

All holes are graded according to their difficulty, using something called 'par'. A par is the amount of shots that a player is expected to take in order to complete the hole. For example, a short hole, anything under about 200 yards, is usually known as a 'par 3' because it should take three shots: one to get to the green, one to get near the hole and one to get the ball in the hole.

Anything above that but still less than about 450 yards will require a drive off the tee, an approach shot to the green, one stroke to get near the hole and one to sink the ball. That's a par 4. Some holes are even longer, requiring a big tee-shot and two approach shots before the two shots on the green. This would be a par 5. Some countries are extending their holes even further and creating par 6 holes, but they're not very common so that was the only mention they're getting in this book. Now, let's get back to this hypothetical round of golf because your hypothetical partner, Nigel, is tapping his feet and tutting impatiently.

This first hole is a 380-yard par 4, so remember that you've got four shots to put the ball in the hole. Any more than that and your scorecard will start to read scarier than a Stephen King novel.

Now, it's not unheard of for a golfer to hit the ball from the tee and land it straight in the hole, but it's highly unlikely, especially on a hole of this length. On a par 4, the aim is to hit the ball a long way with the first shot, to put it on the putting green with the second, to get it near the hole with the third and to put it down the hole on the fourth.

You'll notice different shades of grass on the picture. The shaded areas represent what we call 'the fairway'. This area will always be made up of short grass and it's where you want the ball to go. A ball on the fairway is nice and simple to hit, you see, so think of your ball as a car, these dark areas as the road and the light areas surrounding it as, well, not the road. The lighter areas with shrubs around the fairway are the 'rough', which could be anything from longish tufts of grass to a mass of near-jungle terrain. Either way, you really don't want to put the ball in it. In the same way that a raised ball is easier to hit, a ball obscured by grass is a nightmare to connect with. Even the best golfers run the risk of swinging the club into the ground or a heavy tuft of foliage, ruining the shot completely. You see, rough doesn't just lead to a simple case of losing vital yardage, it means that you have to change your club. The big heavy driver that you use to get enormous distance on the tee-shot is virtually useless in the thick stuff because the grass wraps itself around the head and cuts the power dramatically. One of the thinner iron clubs has to be utilised to cut through the obstacle, so you're not just in the wrong place, you're doomed to a recovery shot that won't be able to take you significantly closer to the hole.

So, let's go back to the tee. You take a big swing with the club and hit the ball hard. It makes a lovely 'thwock' noise and whizzes off through the air, straight down the middle of the fairway. This is a perfect shot. Some people can get hung up about the length of their tee-shots, always trying to squeeze a few more yards out at the risk of compromising their aim, but golf is a game of percentages. Get the ball away and get it down the fairway and you can't go too far wrong. In this case, you've hit it approximately 200 yards and it's all looking good. Your opponent, Nigel, drives the ball just as hard, but without the same accuracy, and it lands in the rough over to the right of the fairway, slightly behind your ball.

It's not impossible to put the ball down the hole from here, but again, it's incredibly unlikely. A far more realistic expectation is simply to put the ball on what is known as 'the green'. The green is a near-sacred area of the golf course, carefully cultivated and protected. It boasts a fine layer of grass so short that you could comfortably play snooker on it and somewhere within its borders will be a flagpole, sticking proudly out of the hole. You and Nigel amble down the fairway with your golf bags, separating to stand by your balls. Even though Nigel played the last shot, he will now have to go first because he is furthest away from the hole.

Remember, Nigel didn't manage to hit the fairway so his ball is in a patch of ankle-deep grass. This means that he is unlikely to get as much distance on his shot and that it will be very difficult to control. He pulls out a smaller club and takes an almighty swing at it. There is an ugly, tearing noise as iron connects with flora. The ball pops up in the air, pursued with extreme prejudice by a large lump of grass and soil. Nigel grimaces, but it's not so bad. The ball bounces back onto the fairway about 70 yards away from the green. Now it's your turn.

With the far easier task of lifting the ball off the fairway, you can be relatively relaxed. You take out an iron club, used for hitting the ball distances of less than 200 yards, and you prepare to take your shot. As your tee-shot travelled 200 yards, the hole is now about 180 yards away. You take your swing and the ball travels fair and true. It catches a favourable bounce off the edge of the fairway and comes to rest on the outer fringes of the hallowed green. Congratulations. You've made the green in two shots, a 'Green in Regulation' (GIR). GIR is a fancy way of saying that you're on track to complete the hole in the required number of shots. It is always two shots less than the par, so to achieve GIR on a par 5, you would have to hit the green on your third stroke.

Poor old Nigel is still lagging behind, so it's his shot next. From 70 yards, he lofts the ball high into the air and it lands comfortably on the green, some 20 yards from the hole. That's his third shot, while you've only taken two, but you're now the furthest away so it's your go. The play is ordered in this manner for two reasons. Firstly, it prevents the ignominy of one player racing up the fairway and finishing, while the other one hacks his way there in twice the number of shots. No one wants to have to bring a book along to a golf course to keep themselves amused while their hapless partner suffers. Secondly, it adds to the suspense to keep the simplest shots until last when the pressure's really on. There are occasions on the putting green when the nearest ball can be in the way of the furthest ball. If this happens, the ball is removed and replaced with a very small, very flat marker.

The only club that is allowed to be used on the green is the 'putter'. If a greenkeeper ever found you using anything else, he'd be well within his rights to kill you where you stood and there's not a jury in the land that would convict him. Anyone who has ever played 'crazy golf' on a windswept British beach will know what a putter looks like. With a flat iron head on a shortish shaft, it is designed for one thing and one thing only: putting the ball down the hole. There are a number of different styles of putters designed according to personal taste, but they fall into three categories.

The conventional putter is the kind of thing you'll have used on a crazy golf course, nice and simple and used by the majority of golfers. It is designed to be precise and natural-feeling, but the only drawback is that it's very easy to lose control of the aim. Any excessive wrist movement could send the ball off course, so golfers need to hold their nerve when they use it. The longer putter is known as the 'belly putter', allowing the golfer to anchor the club against the abdomen for more stability. What you lose in control and feel, you make up for in safety. Then there's the long putter, otherwise known as the 'broomstick putter'. Bernhard Langer, the German golfer of the 80s and 90s, used to prefer this style, but they're not very popular. The shaft is so long that the best way to operate them is to swing them like the pendulum of a grandfather clock, eliminating wrist movement entirely, but sacrificing an awful lot in comfort. It's all about personal taste, but for the moment it's best to imagine the crazy golf variety.

Now, you're right on the edge of the green, about 30 yards away from the hole, so it's still not going to be easy to put the ball down. Greens aren't always flat, so you have to have a long look at the surface and compensate for any dips or bobbles, as well as judging how hard to hit the ball. There's not much in this world that is more frustrating than the sight of a golf ball gently running out of steam, yards shy of its target. You take your best shot, but you underestimate the terrain and the ball trundles past the hole, stopping about 5 yards away from it.

Behind you, Nigel makes a sympathetic comment, but he can't hide the excitement in his eyes. He may have blown his tee-shot, but he's not out of it yet. This is a par 4, and you've both had three shots. From 20 yards, he lines up his shot, knowing that if it goes in, he'll have scored a par. It misses.

The ball rumbles down the green towards the hole, but it catches the lip and fizzes off at a right angle, stopping a couple of yards away. With a primal howl of frustration, Nigel sinks to his knees, head thrown back to the heavens. That's four shots on a par 4 and he isn't finished yet. He can no longer score a par. He sinks his ball without a murmur of celebration and marks a little '5' on his scorecard. Now it's your turn. Five yards from the hole, you line up your fourth shot. Concentrate. Concentrate. Concentrate. And hit. It seems to take an eternity, but with the bare minimum of fuss, the ball rolls into the hole with an echoey rattle that you'll later describe as your new favourite noise. You've scored a '4', a par. You've done everything that the course designers have expected of you. You've teed off, hit the fairway, reached the green and putted the ball. Exceptional stuff. The only problem is that Nigel won't talk to you anymore. Ah well, them's the breaks.

The clubs

Flushed with success and beaming wickedly at your disconsolate partner, you wander over to the second hole of the golf course. It's a far shorter affair, this one, but that doesn't mean it's any easier. Just 140 yards separate you from the flagpole on this gentle par 3. You seem quite bright, so I'm sure I don't have to remind you that a par 3 should be completed with three strokes of the club. This one has a shortish fairway leading to a nice round green with a hole

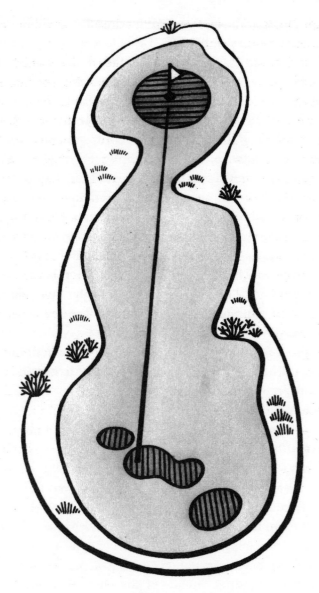

A generic par 3 hole with shorter fairway

stamped right in the middle of it. It's time to learn about golf clubs and how they work.

Golf clubs are like artists' pencils – they're all designed with a specific purpose in mind. When you're drawing a picture and you want a dark line, you use a 4B. If you want a lighter line, you use a 2B, lighter still, an HB. You can probably make an HB pencil leave a mark as gloomy as a 4B if you push on the paper hard enough, but you'll look silly and probably end up breaking the lead. Golf clubs work in a similar way. A driver can hit the ball very hard indeed. Then there is a small selection of wooden-headed clubs that can get a slightly shorter distance. Iron-headed clubs are used for medium distances, with wedges being utilised specifically to get out of bunkers and rough grass. Could you use a driver for the whole course and just adjust your swing accordingly? Well, yes, but you'd look as ridiculous as an artist frantically rubbing away at a sketchpad with the wrong kind of pencil.

A good golfer will always know roughly what kind of distance he can get out of his clubs. If he needs 100 yards, he might select a 9 Iron. For 150 yards, perhaps a 4 Iron will do the job. The lower the number, the further the ball should go. With a big selection of clubs in the bag, there are not many situations that will catch you unawares. Overleaf is a guide to the yardage of most clubs.

Club	Distance in yards (Male)	Distance in yards (Female)
Driver	200–260	150–200
3 Wood	180–235	125–180
5 Wood	170–210	105–170
2 Iron	170–210	105–170
3 Iron	160–200	100–160
4 Iron	150–185	90–150
5 Iron	140–170	80–140
6 Iron	130–160	70–130
7 Iron	120–150	65–120
8 Iron	110–140	60–110
9 Iron	95–130	55–95
PW	80–120	50–80
SW	60–100	40–60
Putter	N/A	N/A

Those figures are only a guide to what should be achievable. Obviously, an awful lot depends on the skill and the physical strength of the golfer in question, not to mention the wind, the weather and the height of your starting point. Hit a ball from a lofted position and you'll find it will go a lot further than you may have expected. Try to hit a ball up a hill and you'll get much less distance than on a flat surface.

Incidentally, you may be wondering what SW and PW are. These are the wedge clubs: the sand wedge and the pitching wedge. We'll have a closer look at them later; suffice to say that they are the preferred clubs for getting out of hazards and for making short distances because of the open face of the club that sends the ball higher into the air.

Now, let's get back to that par 3. You performed best on the last hole, so it's your honour to start first on this one. You check your new list of club yardages and, knowing that it's 140 yards to the hole, you plump for the 6 Iron which should give you somewhere between 130 and 160. You definitely don't want a driver and an iron club will give you a bit more lift than a wooden one. Even so, it's best not to hit this one too hard. In fact, are you sure that you don't want to use a 7 Iron, it might…

Thwonck! What did I just tell you?! You've hit the ball with every ounce of strength you've got, with a 6 Iron no less, and it's gone sailing over the green and into the rough about 30 yards behind the hole. Nice shooting, Tex. Nigel can't contain his glee. Not only are you in trouble, but you've also given him a quick demonstration of what can go wrong. Knowing that you've overshot the mark by some distance, he scales down and picks a 7 Iron out of his bag. With a calm and smooth swing, quite unlike his effort on the previous hole, he sends the ball up into the air and lands it on the green 6 or 7 yards away from the hole. Then he does a bit of a dance, because he's that kind of chap.

You're the furthest away from the hole, so you have to go first. When you're playing out of the rough grass, as you are, you want a club with a nice open head, something that can scoop the ball out of the foliage and send it straight up in the air. A pitching wedge should do the job. It won't go very far, but then you're only 30 yards from the hole. So you don't really need it to, do you? Thwack! You send the ball up and onto the green, a little too far if I'm honest with you, but hey, it's on the dance floor. Nigel watches with interest and then turns to his ball. He's on the green, so he's got his putter out and he sends the ball to within inches of the lip of the hole.

Frustrated, he growls a very rude word indeed and, with his third shot, taps the ball home. He's scored a par, which is absolutely fine, but I think we all know that he could have done even better.

You're still a good 10 yards from the hole, so it's not all over yet. You can hit this one down, can't you? All you've got to do is to take the time to judge the terrain, read the slope of the… oh. Oh, I see. You rush your shot and hit it too hard. It skims past the hole with barely so much as a by-your-leave and you end up having to take a fourth stroke to put it down. Like Nigel before you on the first, you've failed to achieve a par. You've scored a bogey. Still, at least you know how the clubs work, eh?

The obstacles

So, you probably think that you're getting the hang of this now, don't you? Well, we're not there yet, I'm afraid. Let me introduce you to 'hazards'. As if hitting a golf ball hundreds of yards through the air towards a small target wasn't difficult enough, the designers of golf courses around the world have hit upon some cunning ways of making your life even more difficult.

You pick your ball out of the hole and saunter off to the third hole. So far, you and Nigel are neck and neck. A par 4 and a par 3 mean that you should have taken seven shots to get round this far, but you've both taken eight. You need to pick up a shot somewhere and the best place to do that is a par 5. These long ones are terrifying at the best of times. The distance, usually around 500 yards, is one thing, but this hole has some nasty obstacles for you to avoid.

Look at that stream cutting across the fairway about 200 yards down. Horrible, isn't it? Whatever you do, you have to

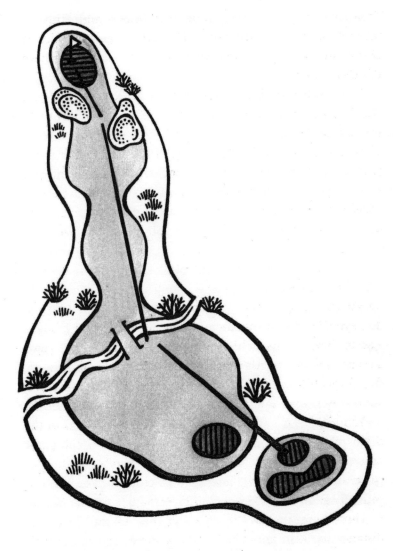

A generic par 5 hole with a long fairway,
a stream cutting across the horizontal
and the green guarded by two bunkers

make sure that you avoid that. And up there, near the hole, do you see those bunkers? You don't want to end up in there either. Don't say I didn't warn you.

Nigel scored best on the previous hole, so it's his honour for the third. He has a very important choice ahead of him. Does he hit hard and try to land the ball on the far side of the stream, risking a watery doom, or does he 'lay up', hitting the ball with less power to ensure that he stops short of the obstacle? How brave does he feel? Well, in this instance, the answer is 'very brave'. He takes out his driver, draws breath and then wellies the ball down the fairway. It flies straight and true and Nigel glows with pride, for he really could not have hit it any better. It bounces once on the fairway, rears up and then falls out of sight. From 200 yards away, carried by the soft mid-morning breeze, you both hear a gentle 'splosh'. Nigel has hit the water hazard.

Water hazards can really ruin a golfer's day. They bring an instant one-stroke penalty and the wretched player must choose whether or not to take the shot again, or to drop the ball behind the water hazard and shoot from there. Either way, Nigel's next shot will count as his third, not his second, and he's no longer a happy bunny. Incidentally, there is another kind of water hazard out there to terrorise innocent golfers and that is the lateral water hazard. Some fairways are flanked on one or both sides by long streams positioned to catch the misguided drive. Now, obviously you can't recover from a lateral hazard by picking the ball out of the drink and positioning it in line with the hole at the edge of the water because it's a straight running stream. The ball must be placed within a club's length of the point that it went awry and a one-shot penalty is imposed.

Being a bit of perfectionist, Nigel decides to take the shot again, but he plays it safe this time and lands the ball 30 yards short of the stream. Thanks to his untimely immersion from the tee, his next shot will be his fourth and you haven't even swung a club in anger yet.

So, what are you going to do? That's right. You're going to learn from Nigel's mistake and you're going to lay the ball up right before the stream. A calmly swung 2 Iron should do the trick, but if you're really being cautious you may even consider a 3 Iron. Basically, you want to do anything to avoid drowning your ball. You take out your club and fire a straight one down the fairway, coming to a stop just behind Nigel's ball. You're the furthest away, so you get to go first, but look what you're aiming at. The hole is still about 300 yards away, but there are sand bunkers guarding it. Do you go for the long shot and try to give yourself an easy chip onto the green or do you lay up again and make sure you miss them? You know what the sensible answer is, but sense is for wimps. You can't spend your life running from danger, you can't exist like a coward in the shadows. There's a time to stand up, a time to stand proud, a time to play chicken with fate and say, 'Yes! Yes, I will go for the long shot, yes I will take on the bunkers!' Now go on! Hit that ball!

Ah … that little puff of golden sand in the distance is a sign, you see. It's a sign that you just landed yourself in the bunker. Sorry about that, I blame myself. I shouldn't have egged you on. Still, let's see what Nigel does, eh? He's already on his fourth shot, so he's not taking any chances. With impressive composure for a man who has already hit the wet stuff once today, he lays up about 20 yards in front of the bunker, 50 yards away from the green. He then takes his pitching wedge and lobs the ball onto the green for his fifth shot. But let's get back to you in the bunker.

Some bunkers are deeper than others. Really nasty ones appear downhill of putting greens and can have a veritable cliff face on one side for you to try to get the ball over. Others are a little more benign, a little flatter and easier to deal with. This is one of the latter, but it's all about the way the ball lands. Just as with grass, the deeper the ball goes in the sand, the harder it is to hit. Sometimes a ball will hit the sand so hard and at such an angle that it will bury itself halfway in. This is known as a 'fried egg'. Thankfully, you haven't got one of those. The ball has impacted on the surface, but has stayed relatively clear. All you have to do is break out the sand wedge and get it back up where it belongs. You're a sensible player, well, you are now after having learnt this important lesson, and you concentrate only on lifting the ball out of the trap. It sails up and bounces onto the green about 10 yards away from the hole, a fine shot.

Nigel, whose putting game really has disintegrated, takes two shots to get the ball down, which makes seven in total. You, purely because I like the cut of your jib, nail it in one, scoring a four on a par 5. Congratulations, you've just claimed your first 'birdie' and I think that means its time to enter the weird world of golf scores.

Scoring
You and Nigel have completed three holes on the hypothetical golf course, so let's have a look at your scores.

	You	Nigel
Hole 1 (par 4)	4	5
Hole 2 (par 3)	4	3
Hole 3 (par 5)	4	7
Total	12 (-)	15 (+3)

As you can see, you have taken 12 shots to complete the three holes, which is exactly what would be expected of a professional player. A par 4, a par 3 and a par 5 add up to 12 and that's precisely what you got. Nigel wasn't quite as fortunate though. A bad first hole and a far worse third hole means that he's behind by three shots. But let's have a closer look at the individual scores. A number of nicknames have sprung up over the years to prevent everyone from having to say, 'I scored an even, then a one over, then a one under,' which would get very tiresome very quickly.

Bogey

If, like Nigel on the first hole, you take one more shot than the par to sink the ball, then you've scored a bogey. Take two more shots, as Nigel did when he took seven strokes on the par 5, and it's a double bogey. Three over constitutes a triple bogey and you could go on, but golf has a far more humiliating level of failure. Anything over a triple bogey demands that you just say the number of strokes you needed.

'Hello Alan, what did you think of the 17th?'

'It broke my heart, Geoff. I went down in ten.'

At this point everyone present would suddenly find something fascinating to stare at on the floor, there would be some awkward coughing and, if they were good friends, someone would change the subject to the weather.

Interestingly, though I'm probably playing fast and loose with the definition of that word, a bogey actually used to mean a par. You see, players would contend that the only thing capable of playing a perfect round would be a 'bogeyman', an invisible opponent of exceptional ability. Therefore, if you could match your imaginary, perfect opponent you would have scored a 'bogey'. Unfortunately, the design of golf balls and equipment improved to such an extent that golfers could drive the ball significantly further than their predecessors. All of a sudden, 'going round in a bogey' wasn't actually as impressive as it used to be. Pars changed to reflect the new equipment and the bogey became A Bad Thing.

Par

If you're playing on a par 4 and you putt on your fourth shot, then you've scored a par, which is Latin for 'equal'. You've completed the hole to a professional standard. Par can also mean completing the course in the required number of strokes, usually 72. Either way, it means that everything is absolutely fine. This also explains why office workers, laying the groundwork for a convenient sickie, will take every opportunity to tell their colleagues that they're a little 'below par'.

Birdie

If a golfer, as you did on the third hole back there, sinks his putt one shot under the par limit, he has scored a birdie. The phrase came into use in the 19th century when an American golfer, Abner Smith, put his second shot on a par 4 right on the lip of the hole. Plonking it down for a three, a rarity in those days, one of his playing partners whooped with joy and declared it to be 'a bird of a hole'. While English slang 'bird' denotes a woman, possibly an extra on an episode of *The Sweeney*, in 19th-century America 'a bird' was a jolly good thing indeed. The name stuck and, due to the importance and popularity of the Atlantic City Country Club where it was coined it quickly travelled the world.

Eagle

On the rare occasion that a golfer manages to put the ball down two shots under par, he will claim an eagle. This doesn't happen very often, but can occasionally be spotted on a par 5 when a golfer with a ferocious drive manages to reach a favourable position on the green with his second shot. From there, he'll be just one shot away from an eagle. It's not unheard of to score an eagle on a par 4, but this would mean a good shot from the tee followed by a 150-yard plus shot to finish. That's a little out of the range of mere mortals like you and me.

Albatross

Continuing the trend of avian nicknames, an albatross is the name given to any hole completed in three shots under the par. In America they don't call it an albatross, they just call it a 'double eagle', but that's nowhere near as interesting. An albatross requires two shots on a par 5, but goodness me, they would have to be great ones. An albatross would need a long drive and then an absolutely inspired 200-yard plus shot to finish and we're beginning to get into the realms of fantasy here, I fear. In fact, according to PGA statistics from 2002 an albatross is ten times as rare as a hole in one. Mind you, there is still something less likely than an albatross out there.

Condor

Complete a hole in four shots under par and you'll pick up a fabled condor. You'll also put your name in the history books because hardly anyone anywhere in the world has ever managed it. A condor requires a hole in one on a par 5, which is practically impossible. The first condor came in 1962 when Larry Bruce clattered his tee-shot through the upper reaches of trees, circumventing the curve of the fairway and landing the ball on the green and down the hole. In 2002, Mike Crean hit a straight condor at the ninth hole of the Green Valley Ranch in Denver, Colorado. A combination of a strong tailwind and the thin atmosphere of the high altitude course gave his ball far more flight than normal and it went down after a journey of 517 yards. However, it is important to note that no one has ever achieved this feat in a professional game. If I were you, I wouldn't hold my breath waiting for it to happen.

Hole in one

If you're fortunate enough to hit the ball from the tee and land it straight in the hole, you'll have scored a hole in one. Many golfers will live their entire lives without having felt the unadulterated joy of hitting one of these magical shots, but don't despair. Golf etiquette demands a balance for pain and pleasure. Hit a hole in one and you're obliged to buy a drink for every single person in the club bar at the end of the round. This is why lots of people prefer to play on weekday mornings. It's just not worth the risk of doing it on a Saturday afternoon. As mentioned earlier, a condor is actually a hole in one on a par 5, but this is the only moniker that gains supremacy. An eagle on a par 3 or an albatross on a par 4 are technically correct definitions, but they would both be described as a hole in one. It just sounds better.

Penalties

There are an awful lot of things that can go wrong on a golf course, and I don't just mean falling in the water hazards. All sorts of laws must be obeyed if a player is to avoid picking up penalties. Here's a few of the most common infractions and what they'll do to your scorecard.

Out of bounds

Although the average golfer will spend much of their time in areas of the course that are some distance from their intended destination, there is a limit to a player's inadequacy. Most holes have fences or hedges or even just a line of stakes to designate their furthest limits. Land a ball over here and you'll be out of bounds. This offence carries a one-stroke penalty and the wretched golfer will have to repeat their shot. Interestingly, this is also the case for a lost ball. Spend any more than five minutes searching for it and it will be declared 'missing in action'. That's a one-stroke penalty as well.

Ball unplayable

It is entirely down to the player to decide what is playable and what is unplayable. There is no obligation to always play the ball from where it lies, which is very good news for anyone who can hit an almost impenetrable thatch of brambles as often as I can. Unfortunately, salvation comes at a cost. Declaring the ball to be beyond help results in a one-stroke penalty. Once the declaration has been made, the player is free to pick it up and drop it somewhere within a two-club radius, but not in the direction of the hole. Unplayable positions could be behind trees, in between the roots of trees or even, in the case of one unfortunate friend of mine, up a tree. I'm still not sure how he managed that.

Ball moves after address

Most golfers will take a little time to prepare themselves for their shot. They'll have a bit of a stretch, check the wind, select a club and then embark on the traditional ceremony of 'addressing the ball'. This doesn't mean designating it with a name and introducing it to your friends – rather it means practising your swing. Most golfers will motion to take their shot, but will stop the downswing just before the club hits the ball. Just to make sure they've got their swing right, you see? You'd be amazed at just how often people screw it up. Any kind of movement of the ball – even if it's just rocked forwards by the change in air pressure – and you're in trouble. Time for a one-stroke penalty and the replacement of the ball on the spot.

Grounding the club in a hazard

When a ball lands in sand, it can be very difficult to hit. This is the point of bunkers, you see. If they elevated the ball and made it easier, everyone would aim for them and you'd have a completely different game. Sneaky golfers will occasionally try addressing the ball in a manner which minimises the effect of the hazard. For example, if you were to lower your club, head first, to a point just behind the buried ball and push down hard, you would lower the surface of the sand, freeing the ball in the process. You would also incur a two-stroke penalty because this is 'grounding the club' and it is cheating. It's not just sand either. Do it in the rough and you'll get exactly the same penalty.

Wrong score on the card

If you get caught lowering the score on your card, you'll be in all sorts of trouble. For starters, you'll be disqualified from whatever competition you are in, but that's nothing compared to the unofficial punishment that will resonate around the clubhouse for years to come. No one likes a cheat. Mind you, if you mess up your scorecard by accidentally inflating your score, you'll be absolutely fine. You can't change it once it's been handed in, but no one will refuse to play with you ever again. In fact, given that you can't count, potential opponents will probably be more eager than ever to play you.

Too many clubs

No golfer can have more than 14 clubs in their bag during a round. The reasons for this are obvious. The more clubs you have at your disposal, the more situations you can react to. You could take 30 clubs in a little golf cart, one for every scenario. By limiting the bag to 14 you can make sure that the playing field is relatively level, so to speak. Golfers who forget this rule do so at their peril. When the mistake is discovered, two strokes are deducted for every hole that was played, but don't panic. There's a maximum of four strokes that can be deducted, although some competitions will disqualify you on the spot, which is the kind of thing that can really ruin your day.

The shots

In the early days of your golfing career, you'll do well to master one kind of shot: the one where you swing the club down and make contact with the ball. Don't laugh, I still can't do it properly every time. Watch a professional tournament though, and you'll see all kinds of special techniques, honed by golfers over the years with the aim of making the ball do exactly what they want it to, and not what *it* wants to. Let's have a look at some of the most recognised styles of shot.

Drive

The drive is the shot that sets your stall out for the hole. Pick up the driver, drop the ball on the tee and then open up for maximum power. It's all about the smoothness of the swing and the composure of the golfer. That's what they tell me, anyway. Some players can drive a ball 300 yards in a straight line, but we can't all be like that, can we? The drive will tell you all you need to know about the mental strength of a player. A nice, straight hit on the 18th on the fourth day of a major tournament tells you that you're dealing with one tough cookie. A wild hook off the tee from the first and it's usually a sign that someone's had too much coffee.

Chip

In a perfect world you would always make the green when you wanted, gently lofting the ball 100 yards and seeing it land in position. Welcome to the real world. In the real world, you're more likely to miss the green by something irritatingly close like 10 or 20 yards. In this case, you want to chip the ball onto the dance floor and give yourself the best chance of putting it in the hole on your next shot. The chip is one of the easiest shots to learn because there's barely any backlift and you'll be using one of the more open-faced wedge clubs. Having said that, mastering the ability to judge distance is no walk in the park. Most chips shots are swiftly followed by an inventive selection of swearwords as the ball sails over the hole or falls frustratingly short of the green.

Pitch

This is a similar kind of shot to the chip, but with more distance and a higher flight path. Generally speaking, you'd be looking to pitch if you were 40–50 yards from the hole and you wanted the ball to go straight up and come back down again without rolling straight off the green. Pitch shots are the domain of the wedges and occasionally the high-numbered irons. Incidentally, these kinds of shot are known as a golfer's 'short game'.

Flop

One of the riskiest but most interesting shots available to a golfer is the flop. Executed correctly this shot should lift the ball high into the air, advancing it only a short distance and getting it to come down to a dead stop on the green. Using a wedge, the clubface must strike the bottom of the ball and lift up, otherwise you'll spank it for miles and everyone will laugh at you. Some golfers can put spin on these shots, but that's just showing off.

Punch

Sometimes a golfer just needs to keep the ball as low as possible. This could be because he's landed in the rough or underneath some overhanging branches, or it could be because there's a horrendous crosswind on the 4th that could take a ball and land it on the 15th. Either way, this is the time for a punch shot. It's a good shot for a middle-range iron, but it requires excellent technique. The golfer needs to lean over the ball in order to prevent it rising up to the heavens.

Draw/fade

Many holes are constructed with what is known as a 'dogleg'. This is where a straight fairway suddenly angles off and continues in a different direction, making a straight shot impossible and looking, from above at least, like a gigantic dog's leg. Usually there will be trees in place to prevent a player from simply blasting over the corner. This means that the average golfer will have to take one shot to get to the corner and then another to aim towards the green. That is, of course, unless he knows how to draw or fade.

This incredibly difficult but invaluable skill is one of the most beautiful sights on a golf course. With the correct foot positioning, the ball can be made to travel slightly to the right of centre before gradually veering off to the left (draw) or start off by heading left and then circling off to the right (fade). Master the amount of angle and power and you'll find that doglegs are as much of an obstacle to you as stairs are to that dalek with the jet thrusters.

Many inexperienced players find that they are fitted as standard with something similar to this when they start, except that it's called a hook or a slice. This is when the ball curves far more severely than expected, either right-to-left (hook) or left-to-right (slice), and it tends to occur when you're just trying to hit the ball in a straight line. Well, it does for me anyway.

Shank

Everyone shanks the ball at some point. Everyone hears that horrid clanking noise, the telltale sign that something has gone horribly wrong. Even Tiger Woods shanks occasionally. The intention of every golfer is to bring the club down so that the clubface connects perfectly with the ball. When the club is off target by just a centimetre or two, there is a risk that you will hit the ball with the curved bit of metal connecting the clubhead to the shaft, which is known as the hosel. That curve can send the ball off in all kinds of directions, except for the one you had in mind. Usually, for a right-handed golfer anyway, it will go hard right. Shanks are just horrendous.

Miscellany

Caddies

Han Solo had Chewbacca, Batman had Robin and Dick Cheney had George W Bush. Everyone needs a sidekick and golfers are no different. Sometimes it's nice to have someone in your corner to dispense kind words and good advice, but more often than not, you just want someone to carry your bag. Those things get pretty heavy.

The caddy first appeared in Britain in 1561 for precisely this reason when Mary, Queen of Scots took young French soldiers out on the golf course with her. Those soldiers were 'cadets', hence the eventual colloquialisation. Poor old Mary couldn't keep her head, but her rejection of heavy lifting gave the sport that she loved a valuable legacy. The caddy was born.

At club level the caddy could be construed as something of a luxury, a golf cart with personality, if you will. In the professional game, however, the caddy is invaluable. The relationship between a golfer and a caddy must be close and, at the top level of the game, they will often be employed and salaried directly by the professional. Caddies are there to advise the golfer on strategy, to aid the golfer with technique, to provide moral support and to do all the annoying things that players hate doing, like filling out the scorecard and, yes, carrying that bag. Professional caddies will be excellent golfers in their own right and will usually put in a few rounds at a course before a competition is played there. They will be their employer's right arm, metaphorically at least anyway.

But before you start worrying yourself about questions of servitude and morality, let me tell you this: almost anyone who is anyone in golf used to be a caddy. It's the traditional apprenticeship scheme for the industry, allowing young players to hone their skills on the course without having to pay enormous membership fees, enabling them to learn their trade and gain experience and, most importantly, earn a bit of money at the same time. At the lowest level, caddies will have to survive on tips from grateful players, but as they rise through the ranks the potential for earnings goes through the roof. In fact, in 2008, the highest paid sportsman in New Zealand was Steve Williams, Tiger Woods' caddy, who was picking up approximately 10 per cent of everything his employer earned which was, as you can imagine, rather a lot.

Handicap

Golf is the only game where it is possible for an amateur to play a professional on a relatively level playing field. This is because of the handicap system that allows players to be graded according to their recent performances.

To put it at its most simple, if you generally go round the golf course taking 10 shots more than the par, which would usually mean you have a round of 82, then you'll have a handicap of 10. Take 20 more shots than the par and you'll have a handicap of 20. The lower the number, the better the golfer. Players who can generally go round a golf course in par are known as 'scratch' golfers and should probably consider turning professional.

Golf handicaps are calculated by the administrators at golf courses. They are the source of much consternation for golfers who will often spend the rest of their lives trying to bring the number down, commonly known as 'working on my handicap'. In the UK the maximum handicap for a male is 28. For a female it's 36. Anything more than that and, like me, you'll have to accept that your main handicap is your own inability to swing a golf club properly.

Of course, this system is only used if you're playing stroke play, the only style of golf discussed so far in this book. If you're playing the hole-by-hole game of match play (see page 56), it does get a little more complicated. In match play every hole on a golf course is ranked in order of difficulty from 1 to 18, with 1 being the hardest. A golfer with an 18 handicap will have one extra stroke on every hole. A golfer with a 10 handicap will have 10 extra shots, but only on the 10 hardest holes. The other eight would have been taken at their face value, the punishment for being a good player.

Etiquette

People play golf for lots of reasons. It's fun, it's social, it's a bit of exercise and it's a chance to get away from the stress of normal life and hit balls really, really hard and we all need a bit of that. The last thing that anyone wants is to have their day ruined by inconsiderate herberts who haven't got the faintest idea of how to behave on a golf course. Despite the best efforts of certain spectators golf is still a civilised affair and that's something to cherish. Here's a few tips on how to avoid the wrath of your fellow players.

- **DON'T** Talk during someone's backswing. Golf is a game of concentration and composure and if someone starts chuntering on about the weather as you prepare to strike the ball, most golf clubs will allow you to retaliate by pulling their arm off and beating them to death with the wet end. It says so in the official rules...

- **DON'T** Shout things at the ball after you hit it. Bellowing 'get in the hole!' at the top of your voice might be acceptable in the red states, but not only will it annoy other golfers around you, it will quickly mark you out as a cretin.

- **DON'T** Run the risk of braining your fellow golfers. If you shank a ball towards a group of players in front of you, you must shout 'Fore!' to alert them to the danger, although you really shouldn't be swinging until everyone has moved far enough up the fairway to be out of range. Wait until everyone is a safe distance behind you before you swing the club, because otherwise you'll take their teeth out. It's also worth being careful when you practise your swing. Though there's nothing quite as funny as the sight of someone inadvertently driving a hidden pebble at their partner, ambulances have a habit of leaving dirty great tyre-tread marks all over the fairway.

- **DON'T** Hold up other players. If you're hacking through the course at a snail's pace, you can always wave them through ahead of you. Not only is it a nice thing to do, but if you think golf is difficult, you should try it with a large group of fuming observers standing behind you and tutting your every move.

- **DON'T** Stand there for an interminable amount of time testing the wind, addressing the ball and taking practice swings. They might do it on the telly, but that's their job and there's hundreds of thousands of pounds riding on it. Your international ranking is not at stake, so get on with it.

- **DO** Repair any damage you cause to the course. If you thwack an almighty lump of turf out of the rough, go and retrieve it and press it back into place. Any divots on the fairway should also be pushed back in as if nothing ever happened. Imagine how angry you'd be if you hit the perfect drive and it landed in the crater of someone else's incompetence.

- **DO** Remember the brand of the balls you are using. It saves lots of time and arguments later when you and your partner land in roughly the same place. Of course, I barely need to mention that it prevents people from changing balls halfway through a hole. Only a cad and a bounder would consider such duplicity.

- **DO** Consider the location of your shadow, particularly on the putting green. Any kind of movement can put a golfer off his game, so be aware that the stretched silhouette of you absently picking your nose is unlikely to aid your partner's performance.

- **DO** Stay off the putting line. The imaginary line that connects the ball to the hole must be kept clear. If you stomp across it before your partner plays his shot, your footprints could cause deviations in the soil that knacker his chances of putting the ball down.

- **DO** Check the dress code for the club before arriving. There are some golf courses that will allow you to turn up in flip-flops, a Hawaiian shirt unbuttoned to the navel and a big cowboy hat, but it's not acceptable at all of them. Most clubs will require sensible slacks and proper golf shoes – basically anything that avoids fostering the feeling that you've just walked in from a barbeque on the beach.

Golf carts

Carts are a contentious issue for many golfers. Ask around and you'll find that many players see them as a cop-out, or a crutch for the very lazy player. Golf is supposed to be about getting outdoors and having a bit of a walk, they argue. Unless you're very old or carrying an injury, you really shouldn't bother with a mechanical aid. Of course, there are also those who think this to be palpable nonsense, reactionary tripe from the ageing members of a dusty establishment. Carts are easy, they're fun and they stop you from getting that throbbing ache down the back of your calves when you sit down after 18 holes. Whichever school of thought you belong to, here's a few ground rules to keep your club membership intact.

- Keep your arms and legs inside the cart when in motion. I know, I know, it's not a roller coaster and you're not going fast enough to lop off a limb should you drive too close to a tree, but it is quite possible to snag a shoelace or a loose piece of clothing in the wheel. It's not unknown for people to break ankles this way and that will put a really quick stop to your game.
- Don't corner too quickly. Although some carts are fitted with seat belts, very few people use them and the last thing you want to do is to flick your partner out of the cart and down a hill. Well, maybe not the 'last' thing. Especially if he's winning at the time. Actually, I shouldn't joke.

Apparently several people have been killed like this. How embarrassing.

■ Many golf courses have specific pathways for the golf carts and ban them from travelling anywhere else. This is because the tyres can make a God-awful mess of the fairway. And don't even think of taking them anywhere near a hazard or a green – they'll chase you to the city limits for that kind of behaviour.

■ Some golf courses have a 90-degree rule, which means that you can drive your cart up the path alongside your ball and then cut across the fairway at a 90-degree angle to approach it, park the cart, play the shot and then get back on the path, again at a 90-degree angle. It's really quite easy, isn't it?

■ They're not dodgem cars. Yes, they're a similar size. Yes, when you're with your mates there's a temptation to regress back to being 11-year-olds. And yes, personally I'd give anything to have a golf cart rally, but it's just not allowed. The carts are very fragile and you'll have a lot of explaining to do if you have to put it back together with sticky tape and push it back to the clubhouse. Don't even think about getting the cart near the water hazards. Despite repeated attempts to prove the contrary, they just don't float.

Nerves and yips

As explained earlier, and as you'll hear from everyone who has ever played the game at any competitive level, you can only get so far in golf with talent and technological advances. The best players will always be the ones in the greatest control of their nerves and emotions. With so much riding on every shot, it's difficult for some players to keep themselves composed.

Many golfers will tell you that the hardest shot of all is the first shot from the tee, especially if you're the first player up. With everyone excited and eager to get things underway, you'll have the undivided attention of your opponents and that's just about enough scrutiny to rattle your nerves like a train full of cutlery. In the same way that a footballer likes to make a few simple passes to get a feel of the ball before they begin to open up with the flash stuff, golfers always want to get a good, safe tee-shot away down the fairway to settle themselves in. Clattering one into the rough from the start can often lead to a slow but steady disintegration in performance.

Most players will suffer from this syndrome at one time or another, but some wretched men and women go on to suffer the dreaded 'yips', a horrendous condition where the body involuntarily flinches and twitches on the putt shot. The yips have destroyed the career of many an aspiring champion and even the best have had to battle it at one time or another. Bernhard Langer, the German player I mentioned earlier, had a terrible time of it, which explains his decision to switch to the long 'broomstick' putter that helps to negate the problem. Despite a string of tournament wins, Langer is most famous for the moment when he 'yipped' in the 1991 Ryder Cup, missing a simple five-foot putt that would have retained the trophy for the European team.

There is a theory that the yips are merely a symptom of ageing, particularly in muscles that have been over-relied upon for too long, though others maintain that they are a product of simple nervousness. Sometimes, all a player needs to do is to break down his action and rebuild it again from the start, but that's easier said than done when your career relies upon continued success.

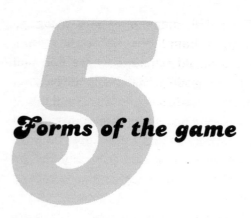

Forms of the game

Stroke play

The game of golf described up until now in this book is stroke play and is the most common form of the game. Essentially, it means that every stroke is recorded on the scorecard, so the final result is dependent on consistency and concentration. Screw up just one hole really badly and you put the entire round at risk. As discussed earlier, players with a handicap remove it from the final scorecard to calculate their final score. Most major competitions are stroke play, usually spread over four days with all of the scores added together to calculate the final winner. Screw up one hole in this game, and you've blown four days of work. In the event of a tie, stroke play games are resolved with a play-off hole.

Match play

The second most common form of golf is the match play game. Here, instead of competing for supremacy over the entire course, the players fight it out hole-by-hole, recording only individual victories. Play a par 4 and secure a birdie while your opponent only makes par and you will win the first hole.

The margin of victory is entirely unimportant; it is enough to say that you are 1 up. If you both hit bogeys on the second, then it's no disaster. You would simply draw the hole and move on to the next one still leading by 1. Spank the ball into the water three times on the fourth, land the lay-up in the sand and go down in 15 and it means nothing to your eventual score. It will almost certainly mean that you will lose the hole, bringing the score back down to 'all square' again, but that's it. What would have ruined your day in stroke play is entirely retrievable in match play.

Match play golf is fascinating because the players are inclined to ignore their natural game and respond to the failings or otherwise of their opponents. If your partner slams his tee-shot into the rough, how eager will you be to play a risky shot? Not very. You can take your time laying up while he hacks it out in the rough, safe in the knowledge that he is the one under pressure. Likewise, all the composure and diligence in the world will mean nothing if he plonks one into the cup from 100 yards. It's less of an endurance race, more of a duel.

Most Major competitions are stroke play, but the Ryder Cup, arguably the most prestigious of all competitions, is match play, in pairs and in teams.

Foursome

Stop giggling. A foursome is a thoroughly decent way of playing the game, although poor performance can lead to some pretty ferocious arguments. The four players split into teams of two, with only one ball for each side. The partners take it in turns to play their shots in either stroke play or match play. The good news here is that if you hit a bad tee-shot at least you're not the one who has to get it back on the fairway. Mind you, the bad news is that if you hit a bad tee-shot, you're not the one who has to get it back on to the fairway, if you know what I mean. This is how the arguments start.

Fourball

Given the amount of strife that must have been caused by foursomes, it is no surprise that someone came up with the fourball. This is almost exactly the same idea, but each player has a ball and their own score. The lowest score for each pair is the one entered at the end of every hole and, again, this can either be in match play or stroke play. It's a team game, but at least one person's inadequacy can't drag his team-mate down as well.

Stableford

Invented in the 19th century by Dr Frank Stableford, this is the only conventional form of golf where a higher score is a good thing. Points are awarded for performance on each hole, according to the number of strokes the player takes to finish either over or under the par.

Points awarded per stroke in the Stableford game	
Strokes	**Points**
2 strokes or more over	0
1 stroke over	1
Par	2
1 stroke under	3
2 strokes under	4
3 strokes under	5
4 strokes under	6

Stableford golf is still played here and there around the world, but it is something of a novelty. The only PGA tour event to use it was cancelled in 2007 after a run of 21 years, so you won't see much of it on the television. In a way, it's something of a shame as it favours the weaker players who can just abort the hole on a double bogey without losing too much ground on their opponent. When you're really not very good at golf, it's reassuring to know that you can't completely wreck your afternoon with one bad spell.

Skins

Skins is a really good way of losing a lot of money. Like match play, players compete on a hole-by-hole basis, but with a cash sum as the prize for each hole won. Let's say that we were playing for £10 a hole. If you won the first hole and I won the second, we'd be even. If you won the third, the fourth and the fifth, I'd owe you £30. Simple? Almost. When a hole is tied, the wager is rolled over on to the next one, so you're playing for £20 on the seventh. Tie it again and the eighth is worth £30. And, if you think that's fun, you should try replacing the money with shots of alcohol. Actually, don't do that. No one likes to see vomit in the bunkers.

In the professional game, wagers are replaced by prize money. The first big skins game was in 1983 when Jack Nicklaus, Tom Watson, Arnold Palmer and Gary Player competed in a big-money, televised event. Player won the competition, which went on to become an annual fixture in the golfing calendar until 2009, when it was postponed due to poor economic conditions.

The competitions

The Ryder Cup

If you're reading this and wondering why it took you so long to discover golf, don't worry. No one can encapsulate the wisdom behind the saying 'better late than never' more accurately than English entrepreneur Samuel Ryder. The cricket-playing 'penny seed' magnate went 50 years of his life without ever playing a round and he ended up as the name behind one of its most exciting competitions. It was a friend of Ryder's who, in 1908, recommended the sport to him as a way of getting a bit more fresh air in his lungs. Ryder was instantly smitten (by the game, not his friend), joining the local club and swiftly bringing his handicap down to single figures. His company sponsored a number of high-profile competitions, but it was an international match at Wentworth in 1926 between a team of Americans and a team of British and Irish players that really caught his eye. Ryder was delighted with the success of the competition and decided that it should be a regular event. He went out and bought a £250 gold trophy and, the following year in Massachusetts, it all got going. Annoyingly, the Americans won.

As explained earlier in the book, the Ryder Cup began as an Anglo–American contest before the continued dominance of the Americans forced the inclusion of a new wave of talented European types. It really was embarrassing back in the day. In the 22 tournaments preceding the change, Great Britain and Ireland won on just three occasions. Now the two 12-man sides are relatively well balanced, which means three days of top-class, competitive golf. Over the course of the tournament, the two teams will compete in a series of match play events: foursomes, fourballs and singles. The first day sees four fourballs and then four foursomes, with the players chosen by the team captain, a pattern which is repeated on the second day. The final day sees all 24 players in action against each other in a run of 12 singles games. A win garners a single point for the team, a tie is worth a half. At the end of the tournament, the team with the highest points wins – it's as simple as that.

Playing in a Ryder Cup is an honour for any golfer, but to be chosen as captain is the greatest accolade that can be achieved in the game. Although the first eight names on the team-sheet are decided by the rankings, the next four spots can be filled with 'captain's picks' allowing the inclusion of wildcard players picked on form, temperament, personality or desperate hope. The captain must also choose the running order of play, deciding whether to throw the best players into the fray from the start or save them for the end in hope that the weaker players hold out.

The Ryder Cup is held every two years, with the venue alternating between America and Europe. Since the postponement of the 2001 competition following the 9/11 attacks, it has always been held in an even-numbered year.

Home advantage is very important in this, the most emotional of competitions. American fans tend to be a little more raucous than their cousins on the other side of the pond and it's not unknown for golfers to be booed or mocked as they go round the course. That inane shout of 'Get in the hole!' takes some getting used to as well. Still, the more they misbehave, the sweeter the taste of victory at the end, eh?

Actually, it was the misbehaviour of the American players themselves in 1999 which was seen as a contributory factor to Europe's three successive wins in 2002, 2004 and 2006. The Brookline event, one of the closest in the history of the Ryder Cup, should be remembered for generations for the stunning American comeback, but you'll not find many Europeans who see it that way. Late on the final day, Justin Leonard's 40-foot putt on the 17th sparked scenes of unrestrained jubilation as American team-mates, caddies, players' wives and supporters alike bounded onto the green to celebrate a famous victory, a quite understandable display of emotion with only one minor problem. They hadn't actually won. Poor old José María Olazábal still had a shot left, a tricky 20-footer. If he holed that, the game would continue to the 18th. Now, 20-foot putts are difficult at the best of times, but you try nailing one when hundreds of over-excited Americans have just thumped up and down all over the playing surface. Olazábal, quite understandably, missed, but if the Americans were looking for a way to gee up future European teams, they had certainly found it.

The Majors

Of all the golf tournaments, and there are many, four stand out as the most prestigious. They are 'the Majors' and to win just one will cement a golfer's place in history. To win all four in one season would give them the fabled 'Grand Slam', but to date, no golfer has ever been quite that successful. Bobby Jones won the old version of the Grand Slam, the two Opens and the two Amateur Opens in 1930, but no one has ever taken both Opens, the Masters and the PGA Championship in the same year. In 1934, Ben Hogan won the first three but was prevented from having a crack at the last by overlapping dates and primitive transatlantic transport links. Since then, Tiger Woods has been the nearest, winning all four, holding all four at the same time, but not quite in the same season. Woods failed to win the first Major, the US Masters, but won the next three and then won the Masters the following year.

All Major golf competitions, and indeed many of the standard tournaments, have a merit-based method of cutting down the competitive field as the event progresses. This is known as 'the cut'. At the end of the second day's play, the only golfers who can progress to the final two rounds are those within ten strokes of the leader. Therefore, if the leader is -7 (seven under par) overall on his two rounds, anyone up to +3 can continue, but a +4 will spell the end of their weekend.

The US Masters

The first Major of the year is always the US Masters, held at the Augusta National Golf Club on the weekend of the second Sunday in April. It is the only Major to remain in the same location year in, year out, and when you see the golf course you'll know why. Augusta is simply gorgeous. Lined with old oak trees and huge banks of flowers, it goes into full, spectacular bloom in the spring, just in time for the TV cameras to turn up. Without getting too botanical, the par 5

13th hole in particular is an exceptional piece of landscape gardening in anyone's book. But that's enough of all that.

The US Masters is a strictly invitational tournament with a small field of competitors, at least in comparison to the other Majors. The top 50 players in the world rankings are always invited, along with former winners of recent Majors, reigning amateur champions and the occasional wildcard chosen by the members of Augusta National Golf Club, an elite collective in itself.

Like all of the Majors, the US Masters lasts for four days, with the stroke play scorecards running on aggregate for the duration of the tournament. The man with the fewest strokes takes home the title. In the event of a tie, there is a tense play-off to decide the winner.

Every champion receives a green jacket, presented to them by the previous winner, and their victory entitles them to play in every future tournament. This is why you could still see the great Arnold Palmer plodding around the course as recently as 2004. Of course, the organisers eventually step in to prevent the field getting clogged up by octogenarians, but not before the younger generation have had a chance to see the stars of yesteryear in their full, albeit creaky, flow. Don't worry though, the legends over-wearied by age are often given the honour of striking the first ball of the tournament, so that's alright.

Another tradition is for all the caddies to be dressed in white jumpsuits, with green caps and a big number on their front. Up until 1982, golfers were only allowed to use club caddies, who were almost always black. Given Augusta's reluctance to allow black members and that 'Caucasians Only' PGA rule, there used to be something a little discomforting about this course. Still, things have certainly changed now, aided enormously by the success of Tiger Woods in 1997. It's pretty difficult to believe in any kind of white superiority when there's a black kid out there spanking the field by a clear 12 shots. For that one extraordinary day, if nothing else, Augusta deserves a special place in the heart of any golf lover.

The US Open

The US Open is the second of the four Majors on the golfing calendar. Unlike the US Masters, the venue switches every year, taking in famous courses like Bethpage State Park in New York and Torrey Pines in California. It takes place in mid-June, with the final round always scheduled for Father's Day in the USA, a nice little touch, I'm sure you'll agree.

The US Open is the only one of the Majors not to finish with a sudden-death tie-break. Instead, the tied players are invited back for a fifth round on the Monday and the title is decided on that performance. In 2008, even this wasn't enough to separate Tiger Woods and Rocco Mediate. They went through the fifth lap of 18 holes, finished tied again and were eventually separated by a sudden-death tie-break hole. Tiger Woods won, but you've probably guessed that already.

As the name suggests, the US Open is open to anybody, but before you rush for your golf bag and book the tickets across the Atlantic in search of fame and fortune, there are still a few obstacles. For starters, you need a United States Golf Association (USGA) handicap of less than 1. Then you need to come through a series of qualifying rounds held on local courses across the country. Succeed there and you reach a secondary qualifying round played out at a number of golf courses across the world. Win that and you're in. It's ... erm ... as easy as that.

Of course, if you're already a practising professional, you may not need to go through all of that rigmarole. Any winners of the US Open from the last ten years are automatically in, as are winners of any of the other three Majors from the last five years. Added to them are the top 30 from the last year's PGA Tour, the top 15 from its European counterpart and the top 50 from the world rankings. That usually gets everyone who's anyone, but should any of the previous year's competition's top 15 still not make it, they'll be added to the list as well.

The early years of the US Open were dominated by Englishmen and Scotsmen, but those days have long since passed. From 1926 to 1964, the only winners were American. After South African Gary Player's 1965 victory, only two non-Americans won it until 1994. As with all the American tournaments, there's a lot to be said for home advantage.

The Open

Always held on the third weekend in July, The Open is the oldest and most cherished of all the Majors. It is also the only Major to be held outside of the USA. Like the US Open, it tours the country and is always held at one of the UK's nine most historic, established and respected links courses. Links courses are different to general courses for a number of reasons. For starters, they're always built close to the coast. Traditionally, this was because the land that separated the farmyards from the beaches was so sandy that it was good for nothing at all. What better place to stick a golf course? Links tournaments, because of their proximity to the sea, tend to be windy affairs with changeable, often inclement weather. St Andrews, the generally accepted home of golf and a miserably wet part of the country at the best of times, hosts the competition approximately once every five years. The Open uses a four-hole play-off as a tie-break, resorting to sudden death only if that fails to generate an outright winner.

The original prize for winning The Open back in 1860 was – brace yourself for this – a red leather belt with a silver buckle. It was retired in 1870 when, surely to the delight of everybody else, 'Young' Tom Morris won The Open for the third time in succession and was allowed to keep it. You can only assume that it ended up at the back of his sock drawer with a bow tie, a box of Homer Simpson handkerchiefs and one slightly tarnished cufflink that he could never bring himself to throw away. It was replaced by the Golf Champion Trophy, better known today as the Claret Jug. Every winner's name is inscribed upon the Jug before the official presentation, a tradition that gives us the occasional close-up of a seriously stressed out engraver desperately trying to remember how to spell Padraig Harrington.

There are 156 players at the start of The Open, with the majority qualifying by virtue of their world rankings. Any former champion under the age of 60 on the first day will also be automatically entered, alongside the usual selection of recent Major winners and the top ten from last year's tournament. Joining them is a swathe of qualifiers from a series of regional tournaments. This means that you'll always get a good spread of amateurs free to clatter around the course with some of the biggest names in the world. The leading amateur player is always awarded a silver medal for their achievement, but any amateur who survives to the final day's play is awarded a bronze medal as well. More important than that, however, is the fact that after a sterling performance at The Open, a professional career won't be far away.

The PGA Championship

The final Major of the season is always the PGA Championship and, for that reason, it is known in some circles as 'Glory's Last Shot'. For years, the PGA Championship was held a matter of days after The Open, which made it practically impossible for people to enter both, transatlantic transport not being what it is today. Now, it's held about a month after The Open, so there's lots of recovery time for everyone concerned.

Until 1958, the PGA Championship was a match play event before eventually joining the other Majors as a stroke play tournament. Even now, there is pressure to change the format from TV advertisers well aware that a small group of top-class players will bring in more revenue than a standard tournament. Despite this, it continues as a normal tournament and does very well, thank you very much, regardless. Held at a variety of US golf courses, including the fabulously named Whistling Straits, Wisconsin, and the equally well-monikered Valhalla Golf Club in Kentucky, it attracts some of the best golfers in the world.

Although it is possible for amateurs to play, it's very difficult. Your average golfer would have to win a Major in order to do it and that doesn't happen very often. The field is made up therefore of the top professional players in the game. All former PGA Champions are invited, along with the last five years' worth of winners of the other Majors, the last Senior PGA champion, the leading players in the rankings, last year's lowest scorers and, on the off chance that they haven't already made it, the US Ryder Cup team.

In 2009, the PGA Championship served up one of the greatest shocks of recent years when Korean golfer Y. E. Yang hauled back a two-shot third-day deficit to prevent Tiger Woods from landing his fifth title in the event. It was the first time that Woods had ever failed to win a tournament after having led the pack at the 54-hole mark. Yang was also the first Asian ever to win a Major. Interestingly, Irishman Padraig Harrington, the engraver's nightmare, was in with a chance of landing the Championship, but a horrific eight on a par 3 blew his chances out of the water. That's the danger of stroke play, you see. One bad hole and it's all over.

The PGA Tour

There are no leagues for professional golfers to play in and there are no divisions with promotion or relegation. Instead, the sport exists on huge season-long tours, travelling golf circuses that bring the best golfers possible to as many courses as feasible. Of all of the tours, the PGA Tour is the most prestigious, mainly because of the phenomenal amounts of money on offer for the top performers. It's not all as cynical as it sounds though. The PGA make a point of raising money for local charities in every city they play and the organisational body is strictly not-for-profit. In 2005, they racked up a total of a billion dollars in all-time charitable donations.

Success on the Tour is also measured by money, in this case the total amount of prize money accumulated, a fairly ostentatious way of doing things, but the accepted system regardless. Players have to continue to win in order to stay on the Tour, earning their place in future competitions with their performances in the past. Only the top 125 earners of the year pick up a Tour card for the following season, but there are short cuts. Win a PGA Tour event – and there were over 40 of them in 2009 – and you get a Tour card for two years. Win a

Major and you get one for five years. Win 20 PGA events and that's a Tour card for life. The Tour runs from January to November, taking in golf courses across the United States.

At the end of the season there are a series of prestigious PGA awards handed out to the best players and the best 'rookie' players. Rookies are players who are competing in their first ever Tour. Take a scan down the former winners of the PGA Player of the Year and you'll find all the names you'd expect: Tiger Woods, Tom Watson, Jack Nicklaus, Arnold Palmer and so on. The PGA Tour Rookie of the Year Award is far more interesting. There you'll find players like the Paraguayan golfer Carlos Franco (1999), who never fulfilled his potential, and John Daly (1991), who did, but then spectacularly self-destructed, as you'll find out towards the end of this book.

The European Tour

Because of the lower prize money on offer, the European Tour is seen as the poor relation of the PGA Tour, which is a little harsh but quite understandable. On this side of the Atlantic your humble golfer can win only 60 per cent or so of the money available in the States. Mind you, as the highest earners tend to pick up around €3 million a season, it's not exactly that much of a hardship, is it? Up until 2009, the objective was to accumulate the most money and to win the European Order of Merit, but that changed with the introduction of 'the 'Race to Dubai', a series of competitions leading to a final tournament in the Middle East with an enormous purse of prize money.

In 1998, the European Tour agreed to allow prize money won in the US Majors to count towards their official standings, a move which obviously had a significant effect on the league table due to the much larger sums of cash available on the other side of the Atlantic.

The European Tour is usually the first place that you'll see promising non-American golfers from around the world. The likes of Greg Norman and Nick Price started out here before graduating to the PGA Tour when they had made their name. Even though the name suggests that all competitions are played in Europe, that's not actually the case. Competitions are played all over the world, anywhere from South Africa to Thailand.

Women's golf

Bring up the subject of women golfers at any dusty clubhouse and you'll always find one misguided doofus who'll tell you that it shouldn't be allowed. They'll justify their Stone-Age standpoint with the oft-quoted theory that the word 'golf' is an acronym for the first rule in the book: 'Gentlemen Only, Ladies Forbidden'. This is a wonderfully simplistic idea acceptable only to wonderfully simplistic brains. It is, however, complete bobbins on a number of counts.

Firstly, the game of golf, as you've already discovered, came into existence hundreds of years ago. There were very few Blackberry-wielding marketing men back in the 15th century, so the odds of someone coming up with snappy acronyms in doughnut-fuelled meetings are rather long. By and large, your average 15th-century Scotsman probably had more important things on his mind than laying down the foundations of institutionalised sexism. The name of golf probably came from a bastardisation of the word 'gawf', which was Scottish slang for hitting something.

Henry VIII used to play golf with Catherine of Aragon. Mary, Queen of Scots was one of the first keen female enthusiasts, using all that spare time she had in Scotland. Suggest to either of these fine ladies that they should be off the fairways and back in the kitchen and you'd probably get a pitching wedge where the sun doesn't shine. And I don't mean St Andrews. To read the history books though, you'd never have a clue that women have been playing golf for just as long as men, but the St Andrews Ladies Club was formed in 1867 and there were regular competitions in existence long before the start of the 20th century.

Women's golf has never been in better shape than it is today. The Ladies Professional Golf Association (LPGA) Tour has a higher profile than ever before, the prize money is getting bigger all the time and the equivalent of the Ryder Cup, the Solheim Cup, gets blanket TV coverage from start to finish. A number of women golfers have actually played on the men's tour, most notably the American Michelle Wie. The Hawaiian-born prodigy was the youngest player to qualify for an LPGA event, making the Takefuji Classic in 2002 at the age of 12, incidentally a record that has since been broken by the 11-year-old Ariya Jutanugarn. At the age of 15, Wie was invited to play in the men's Sony Open in Hawaii, only the fourth woman ever to play with men. She missed the cut by just one stroke, finishing at even par after two rounds.

In truth, there isn't an awful lot of difference between the men's and women's games. Men, generally, can hit the ball further, which has the obvious benefit of saving a few strokes. Until a woman arrives who has the driving power of the male golfers, there will always be a gap in the scorecard, but the most important part of the game is, as I said at the start of this book, between the ears. And there's nothing to suggest that, as a gender, women are any better or any worse than men in that department.

The professional game

Live or TV?

Golf fans, young and old, always seem to be split on one major issue. Is the game more entertaining on television or in the flesh? As this debate has been rumbling on for years, I don't think that I've got a chance of resolving it, but here's some of the best arguments from both camps.

TV

Why would you want the inconvenience of travelling anywhere for golf? Unless you're part of a very traditional Catholic family, the queue for the toilets is likely to be considerably smaller in your own home. You've also got better access to tea, coffee and grown-up beverages. Beat that.

FLESH

Are you seriously suggesting that

sitting in your own living room with a cup of tea is more exciting than a seat in the stands around the 18th hole, watching the players approach the green, feeling the tension rise and hearing the crowd roar? If you're at a competition you get to feel like part of the moment, rather than just part of the audience.

TV

Yes, well, a seat in the stands is a lovely idea, but what are the odds of that, eh? Especially at a Major competition like The Open. You'd have to camp outside the course days in advance. At least on TV you know that you'll never miss the action.

FLESH

Actually, although your point about getting a seat at the 18th is a fair one, tickets for golf competitions are relatively cheap and easy to obtain in advance. Tickets for a day at the 2010 Open were available online for just £15, which is considerably cheaper than a Premier League football match, a day at the cricket or even the pay-per-view fee for a big boxing event.

TV

Yes, but what's the appeal of actually being there? Surely you're either just stood at the green watching balls fly through the air at you, or you're stood at the tee watching people blast the ball miles away before packing up and walking off. It all seems a little impersonal.

FLESH

You can follow the golfer along the course, you know? You don't have to just take root and watch the same thing all day. That's the beauty of buying a ticket. You have the freedom to roam around, taking in the scenery, watching the greats from close range, maybe even picking up a few tips. Of course, it does mean actually leaving the house. Are you ok with that?

TV

How dare you, sir! Leaving the house is no challenge, I just need to be properly motivated for the journey. I haven't heard good things about live golf. A friend of mine went to The Open at Sandwich, Kent once and he hated it. He said it took ages to get there and he never really saw an entire hole, just little bits here and there, punctuated with polite applause. He also told me that the highlight of the day was having the good fortune to stand near a bunker while some poor sod spent 12 shots trying to get out, but apart from that things didn't improve until he found the beer tent, where he was able to watch the progress of the competition on television.

FLESH

Well, he obviously didn't choose his location well enough, did he? If he'd have taken the time to do a bit of research, he might have scouted out a few more interesting locations, like the green of a par 3, or the approach to the all-important 18th. That's where it all gets exciting. That's where you see how the world's best players react to stress and pressure. That's where you get to be in the presence of greatness.

TV

Wow, you really like golf, don't you?

FLESH

Yes. Yes, I do.

TV

What about rain?

FLESH

What do you mean, 'What about rain?'

TV

Well, what do I do if it starts to
rain? It never rains in my house.
I'm safe there. Safe.

FLESH

Goodness me, man! Take an umbrella!
Take a risk! There are plenty of
places to shelter, plenty of
shops and refreshment tents,
I'm sure you'll be fine. Besides,
the prospect of getting drenched
just adds to the excitement,
doesn't it?

TV

Well, not really, but ok. I'm
prepared to take a chance, even
though I'd like my point about
convenient conveniences to be
revisited, while I'd also like to
add a further point about the

availability and price of food.
I don't like getting ripped off.

FLESH

Well, bring your own sandwiches
then. Most golf courses will allow
that, though you'd do well to phone
up and check in advance.

TV

Sounds sensible. Ok, but what about
missing out on the flow of the
competition? When I'm in front of
the telly, I can be sure that I'm
not going to miss a thing. I know
that the producers will whisk me
from the 3rd to the 16th if they
think that something more important
is happening. If I'm actually on the
3rd, I'm fairly sure that I won't be
able to get to the 16th until it's
all over. How will I keep up?

FLESH

Why don't you try bringing along a
little portable radio? Lots of golf
fans do that; they find that it
keeps them in touch with all the
goings-on, as well as letting them
know where they should be heading.
They don't miss a thing, they get to

watch the golf live and they get
a bit of exercise to boot. Not
bad, eh?

TV

Not bad at all. Alright Flesh, if
that is your real name. I'll give it
a go. I'll get online and book some
tickets just as soon as I'm finished
watching this...

FLESH

There's no helping some people, is
there?

Pro-celebrity golf

Of course, if the professional game isn't quite enough to float
your boat, there's always the glamorous world of pro-celebrity
golf. The most famous example of this is the Bob Hope
Classic, held every January in California's Coachella Valley.
The competition itself is actually part of the PGA Tour, but
numerous stars of stage, screen and Senate have graced the
Pro-Am over the years, including Hope's close friend Bing
Crosby, the legendary actors Burt Lancaster and Kirk Douglas
and classic crooner Frank Sinatra.

Hope, an English-born comic genius with a string of box
office successes to his name, adored golf, probably because it
was such a rich seam of comedy for him to mine throughout
his career. He once announced that President Eisenhower was
giving up golf for painting because it involved fewer strokes.

President Ford wasn't spared either. 'The last time I played with President Ford he hit a birdie,' said Hope. 'And an eagle, a moose, an elk, an aardvark...'

Hope lent his name to the tournament in 1965 and, despite the fact that he died in 2003 at the extraordinary age of 100, it remains in place, subject to assurances to his family that the competition will continue to raise significant amounts of money for charity. Despite the noble sentiments, a lot of top golfers choose to ignore the tournament because of the distraction of the celebrities and the chaos that their presence causes. With so many extra fans in attendance a normal round of golf can take considerably longer to play, especially given the more informal atmosphere and the tendency of the players to sign autographs before putting.

Nevertheless, the Pro-Am has been responsible for some pretty historic moments. In 1995, for the first time ever, three US presidents, including the then-incumbent Bill Clinton, played together. Clinton, along with George Bush Snr, Gerald Ford, defending champion Scott Hoch and Hope himself, played in an extraordinary fivesome that must have been a horrendously busy day for all the presidents' security men.

Rocker Alice Cooper recalled his attendance at one of the star-studded events, saying, 'I go in there and there's Hope, Ford and Johnny Carson and Bob says "I'm pushing my drive to the right a bit" ... and that's all we talked about. I realised when I walked away that that was Hope and the President and we never once spoke about anything except how to get your right hand square. That just shows you what golf is. It cuts right through anybody's job, anybody's political stance. Anything.'

Five great golf courses

Pebble Beach, California, USA

One of the most beautiful golf courses in the world, Pebble Beach was designed specifically to hug the Californian coastline as much as possible, which means a series of increasingly dramatic backdrops to your game. The Pacific Ocean crashes against the rocks, the spray rises up and drifts over the green – it has to be said that it's all a bit special. It was designed in 1919 by Jack Neville and Douglas Grant and boasts a number of truly awesome holes, particularly in the mid-section.

'If I had only one more round to play,' said Jack Nicklaus, 'I would choose to play at Pebble Beach. I loved this course from the first time I saw it. It's possibly the best in the world.'

Pebble Beach has played host to the US Open on four separate occasions, notably in 1982 when Tom Watson hit one of the all-time great golf shots. Nicklaus, his rival for the championship, saw the tee-shot bounce in the rough and assumed that Watson would bogey the hole. Everyone did. But marooned in rough and stranded above the hole, Watson ignored the advice of his caddy and unleashed an improbable chip that bounced off the flagpole and plopped into the hole for a birdie. He went on to birdie the 18th and lift the trophy.

Pebble Beach is one of the few big-name golf courses that are easily playable for the amateur. Well, it's easy if you've got the money. In 2009, you would have needed about £500 to secure a round, so it's not the kind of thing you'd do on a whim. Mind you, those views make it all worth it when you get there.

The best hole, and this is not definitive because the debate continues to rage, is probably the eighth, but I've fallen in love with the seventh and it's my book so I get the final say. A tiny par 3, it's a little over 100 yards and it goes straight out towards the Pacific. You can tee off with a wedge and make the green, assuming that you're not put off by the sight of the waves, boosted by thousands of miles of uninterrupted fetch, spanking into the rocks behind the green. Best not to hit that shot too far...

Augusta, Georgia, USA

We've spoken about Augusta on several occasions already, but it's always worth going back for another look at this magnificent course. A shoo-in for anyone's top five, it's a splendid-looking course that players and fans can grow more accustomed to every April when the US Masters is held there. In fact, I'd probably watch the coverage even if there was no golf and it was just one cameraman wandering around at random, it's that good. Unfortunately, it's not particularly easy to get a game there.

You see, Augusta is a private club with a curious 300-strong membership of ex-White House politicians, banking magnates and high-ranking corporate bods. A handful of new memberships are given out every few years, but only to those similarly placed in the social strata. There are no female members at all, although the club has insisted that this does not mean an outright ban, just that they will not allow women to circumvent the membership process simply to satisfy the will of the politically correct. A very tidy get-out clause, I'm sure you'll agree.

Augusta is so private that the club bigwigs won't allow it to be represented in computer games and they won't allow it to be rated by the golf associations. Why not? According to the club chairman, 'We don't need a handicap system. Our members already know each other's games.'

You can play there as the guest of a member, but how many former White House high rollers do you know? There are recorded accounts of members who sustain themselves by inviting their mates for a round and taking several thousand pounds off them for the privilege, but I can't see that kind of rampant capitalism aiding the development of a long-lasting friendship.

As a result, the TV coverage of the US Masters is probably as close as the vast majority of us will ever get to playing a round at Augusta. Maybe that's one of the reasons that it always seems special...

St Andrews, Scotland

The home of the Royal and Ancient Golf Club and arguably the home of golf itself, the Old Course at St Andrews is one of the most challenging courses in the world. So much depends on the weather. A mild day with no wind can turn the 'old lady' into a kitten, but when the nasty Scottish weather kicks in, even the professionals will be desperately hoping just to get round in par. It's not much fun for them, but fans of Schadenfreude will while away many a happy hour watching the biggest names in the world go to jelly in the elements.

You couldn't design a golf course like St Andrews these days. Never mind being able to see the bunkers, which more often than not you can't, half the time the rain is so strong that you can't even find your caddy. If you can find him, you'd better hope that he's a meteorological expert because every time the wind changes, his advice needs to swing with it. You literally never know what you're going to get from a round.

The most famous hole is certainly the 17th, a sadistically designed nightmare of a hole that can reduce a grown man to tears within the first two strokes. For starters, there's a bloody great hotel in between the tee and the fairway, so that has to be cleared with the tee-shot or you're in all kinds of trouble. Mind you, even if you do get over the hotel, you still need to find the fairway, an unforgiving mistress that tightens up in the middle leaving absolutely no margin for error. Get that far without having a nervous breakdown and you'll be facing the nastiest bunker in existence, the Road Hole bunker. This borehole into the earth guards the green and sucks balls in just for fun. It has a sheer face so tall that, once you're in it, you can't see out of it. It's been the ruin of too many golfers to mention, but it is good fun to watch from a safe distance.

Valderrama, Andalucia, Spain

The undisputed finest golf course in continental Europe, Valderrama is the only mainland European site ever to host the Ryder Cup, an impressive achievement for a relatively new venue. It was originally designed in 1974 and known as Sotogrande New, but it wasn't until 1984, when Jaime Ortiz-Patino acquired it, that its reputation began to grow. Ortiz-Patino recalled the legendary course designer Robert Trent Jones, the man who had originally laid down the course, to give the whole place the shakedown of its life. Tens of thousands of square yards of earth were moved in, hills were bulldozed, greens were shifted and tees were moved back. When the surgery was complete, Ortiz-Patino had himself a course that could challenge the greatest players in the world, while still being just about playable for your average amateur. Four years later, Valderrama was on the PGA European Tour and in 1997 it hosted the Ryder Cup. Quite a rise to prominence.

Blessed by perpetually good weather, Valderrama is said to be a dream golf course although you won't find many people who have played there. A private members' club, the owners guard it jealously from outsiders. There are a few tee-times available for visitors, with strict dress codes and stern warnings about etiquette. Not for nothing is the atmosphere at Valderrama compared to the oldest and proudest clubs in the UK.

Valderrama's signature hole is La Cascada, the par 5 fourth hole. It's a long, relatively straight affair, but with a narrow, twisting fairway with plenty of rough on either side. Survive the tee-shot and the first drive and you'll find yourself approaching a two-tier green with a large pond to the right and bunkers fore and aft. A powerful, accurate player can reach the green in two, but there are so many pitfalls positioned to trap the over-confident that it might just be worth taking three.

Turnberry, Girvan, Scotland

Constructed in 1906 on the rugged coastline of Ayrshire, Turnberry's Ailsa Course is steeped in history. It doubled as an airbase in the First World War, a training station for young pilots, before being redesigned and reopened in 1951. Its finest hour, however, would come in 1977.

The memorable 'Duel in the Sun', the battle between Tom Watson and Jack Nicklaus for The Open, was one of the most exciting days of golf ever. Sharing the lead at the start of the final day, they played out the final round together, vying for the lead all the way round. Every time one of them edged ahead, the other would raise his game. Watson, 27, showed no fear as he battled away against Nicklaus, ten years his senior. By the 16th, they were tied for the lead, a whopping ten shots ahead of third place and, in the bright sunshine, Watson turned to his rival and said, 'This is what it's all about, isn't it?'

'You bet it is,' smiled Nicklaus. Again, they tied a hole, going into the 17th neck and neck. Then Nicklaus blew a routine putt on the 17th to allow Watson to take a one-shot lead with a well-taken birdie. Watson teed off at the 18th perfectly, leaving Nicklaus with no option but to play a high-risk shot across the bunker. He landed in the rough. Watson then delivered his ball to within two feet of the hole and it seemed as good as over, but Nicklaus still wasn't giving any quarter. He thumped the ball out of the nasty stuff, plonking it on the green 35 yards from the hole. Then, to the absolute astonishment of the crowd, he sent it zipping across the turf and into the cup. The sun-drenched spectators went absolutely bananas. Watson only needed to sink a straight forward putt to win The Open, but two feet may as well be two miles under that kind of pressure. There was so much noise and commotion in the stands that the youngster couldn't take his shot. Then, in a magnificent act of sportsmanship, Nicklaus raised his arm in the air and appealed for calm. Silence fell over Turnberry, Watson stepped up, gave a couple of practice strokes and dispatched the ball as if he was killing time on a putting green. Nicklaus threw his arm around his conqueror and slowly led him off to the scorer's tent to kick his head in … erm, I mean to congratulate him. The Duel in the Sun was over.

Ten great golfers

Jack Nicklaus

Of all the men and women to have played the game, most people would agree that 'The Golden Bear' stands out as the greatest. Ohio-born Nicklaus was a golfing genius, a tactical mastermind who always played his shots with the next one firmly in mind and who rarely, if ever, made a reckless or foolhardy decision. He won 73 PGA Tour events and a whopping 18 Majors, including six US Masters in a glittering career that spanned five decades. Two amateur titles during his time at Ohio University in 1959 and 1961 were notice of a prodigious talent, but nothing could prepare the world for the phenomenal rate at which he accrued titles. Seven in the 1960s, eight in the 1970s and three in the 1980s, including a final US Masters in 1986 at the age of 46. He played his last Major at the age of 65 in 2005. Appropriately enough, it was The Open at St Andrews. After Nicklaus teed off at the 18th, he received a ten-minute standing ovation from the crowd. All in all, it was a bit of a shame that he missed the cut.

Tiger Woods

The biggest star that golf has ever seen, Tiger Woods is responsible for bringing a whole new wave of fans to the game. A powerful and accurate hitter, he was driving the ball so far at one point that some courses began to extend the yardage of their holes in an effort to 'Tiger-proof' themselves against the possibility of some very one-sided competitions. That's how much he scared everybody. Woods burst on to the scene in 1997 at Augusta when he won the US Masters. By 2008, he had won every Major at least three times. Woods' real strength – well, one of his very many strengths – is his composure under fire. Put his back against the wall, ratchet up the pressure, and you can still rely on him putting the ball without blinking. He is also utterly driven, even sending himself to do Basic Training with the American armed forces when he felt that success was making him too complacent and soft. At the time of writing, however, it was unclear whether his career would ever recover from the allegations made against him in 2009.

Bobby Jones

A strange story, this one. Bobby Jones was arguably one of the finest golfers ever to play the game, but he never turned professional and he retired at the age of 28. Jones was a child prodigy, encouraged to play the game by his father, but his rapid rise to stardom didn't come without cost. He piled pressure upon himself, so desperate was he to succeed at all costs, and often lost huge amounts of weight before competitions through the stress. For years he struggled with his temper and failed to make an impact on the game until 1923 when he won his first Major, the US Open, a victory that tore the floodgates asunder. In the next seven years he won another three US Opens, three Opens and five US amateur titles. In 1930, he completed a unique 'grand slam' of the two Opens and the two Major amateur titles. And then he quit. Mind you, he made sure that he left quite a legacy. First he co-designed the Augusta National golf course, then he founded the Masters Tournament, which would go on to become one of the modern Majors. Jones would compete in his own tournament until 1948 when syringomyelia, a paralysing spinal condition, stole his ability to play. He died in 1971.

Ben Hogan

Texan-born Hogan is one of three great golfers all born within six months of each other in 1912, the others being Sam Snead and Byron Nelson (see below). If you do still harbour the feeling that golf has always been a restrictive, establishment pastime, Hogan's story should make you think again. His father's suicide in 1922 meant that he was selling newspapers outside train stations at the age of nine to help his mother with the bills. By 11, he was caddying at the Glen Garden Golf Club. A gifted young player, he missed out on the club's only junior membership, oddly enough to Byron Nelson, who also caddied there. Some lean years on the lower end of the pro-circuit followed, especially as he developed a nasty hook that prevented him from winning a tournament until 1940. You might think that his life gets more cheerful from there, but a hideous car accident in 1949 should have ended it abruptly. Hogan actually would have died had he not thrown himself in front of his wife to protect her. As it was, he ended up with numerous fractures, including a double pelvis break, as well as serious blood clots that would plague him for the rest of his life. Hogan wasn't supposed to walk again, let alone play, but he recovered to win three Majors in 1953, a feat that was known as the 'Hogan Slam'. Not bad for a poor kid from Texas.

Sam Snead

One of American golf's most beloved characters, Snead was a friendly Southern gentleman with one of the sweetest swings in the history of the game. He wore a straw hat, had an infectious grin and was prone to dropping folksy little nuggets of advice to younger players, like his favourite mantra, 'Keep close count of your nickels and dimes, stay away from whiskey and never concede a putt.' He even played holes barefoot because he thought it would improve his balance. Snead won 82 PGA events over the course of his career, as well as 70 others around the world, and he played the game well into his 80s. A natural sportsman, he had such confidence in his abilities that he didn't have to practise as much as other players, even though his putting was often the weakest component of his game. The only blot on his copybook was his failure to win the US Masters, but as he himself once said, 'I must have been playing pretty good and sinking putts when I won those three Masters, three PGAs and the British Open.' I bet someone picked him up on that British Open faux pas though...

Arnold Palmer

Tactics are all well and good, but what the public really wants to see is a player who lives by the seat of his pants. In Palmer, the people had their champion. The Florida-born son of a greenkeeper learnt the game by following his father around his course as a youngster. In 1955, he won the Canadian Open in his rookie season, but it was the 1960s that would define him. He won The Open twice and picked up four US Masters at Augusta, as well as securing a US Open. Palmer was not a man for caution. He liked to take risks and the American people liked to see them come off. More often than not both parties got their desired result. A charismatic and much-loved American hero, he was a popular figure on the circuit, playing in 50 US Masters, his last appearance coming in 2004. If ever one single shot could epitomise a player, it was Palmer's second on the 18th at the 2004 Bay Hill Invitational. When a 75-year-old man is 200 yards from the pin, the last thing you expect to see him do is reach for his driver. Palmer did and he spanked it onto the green as if it was the most natural thing in the world.

Gary Player

Gary Player's father must have known a good thing when he saw it. A gold miner in South Africa, he had to take out a loan to buy his son his first set of golf clubs. Imagine how upset he'd have been if Gary had been rubbish. Fortunately, on his first round of golf ever, the 14-year-old parred his first three holes, setting the bar for his father's dreams of vicarious success at a ludicrously high level. Not that it would matter; Player would eventually become one of the most successful golfers of all time. He is the only player ever to win The Open in three different decades, the first coming in 1959 as a 23-year-old. Mind you, he nearly messed that one up, double-bogeying on the final hole and bursting into tears. Fortunately for him, no one could take advantage. Another victory followed in 1968 before he bagged his hat-trick in 1974. Perhaps his greatest victory came in the US masters of 1978. He began the final day a whopping seven shots off the lead, but birdied seven of the last ten holes to sweep through and win by a single shot. One of the 'big three' of his generation, along with Arnold Palmer and Jack Nicklaus, he was voted Sportsman of the Century in South Africa.

Seve Ballesteros

One of the most beloved golfers in history, Spaniard Seve Ballesteros kicked the doors in on the golfing establishment when he finished second at The Open in 1976 as an unknown 19-year-old. Three years later, he returned to win it outright. Ballesteros might not have had the greatest drive in the game, but his short game was so exceptional that it rarely mattered. He was so good under pressure that he once hit a birdie after ending up in the car park from his tee-shot. A natural risk-taker and a crowd favourite, he excelled in match play events, especially in the Ryder Cup. He was part of the European side on eight occasions, captaining the team to a famous victory at Valderrama in Spain in 1997. As one half of the 'Spanish Armada' with countryman José María Olazábal, he was practically unstoppable. Ballesteros' career was truncated in the 1990s by a series of back injuries that prevented him from adding to his five Majors, but his place in history was already secured. There wouldn't be a youngster in the game as exciting until the arrival of Tiger Woods.

Byron Nelson

The final member of the classic 1930s triple pack with Ben Hogan and Sam Snead, Byron Nelson played for just 14 years, retiring at the age of 34 to become a rancher in his native Texas. Despite his premature departure from the game, he remains one of the most successful players in its history. Indeed, had it not been for World War II and the suspension of competitive play, he would surely have won more than five Majors. Nelson was a terrifyingly reliable golfer who enjoyed his best season in 1945 when he won 11 victories in a row, 18 in total that season, with an average of 68.33, almost four shots below par. No surprise then that when the USGA invented a device that tested golf clubs and balls in laboratory conditions, they named it the 'Iron Byron'. The big Texan also developed what experts refer to as the first 'modern' swing, pushing his physical power into the swing and making the most of the relatively new steel-shafted clubs. After retirement, he became a television pundit and went on to mentor a number of young players including...

Tom Watson

Oddly, for a man whose professional peak came in the 1980s, Tom Watson's greatest moment was almost in 2009 when he so nearly became the oldest winner of a Major in the history of the game. Within weeks of his 60th birthday, the veteran American led the way through the second and third days and was actually one shot in front on the final hole. Sadly for anyone who loves an upset, he bogeyed the 18th and then lost the subsequent play-off to Stewart Cink. Ah well, at least the near miss served as a reminder of one of golf's finest talents. Watson won eight Majors in his career, including five victories in The Open. He enjoyed some epic battles with the likes of Jack Nicklaus, was coached by the aforementioned Byron Nelson and dominated the PGA Tour throughout the 1980s. Watson was a fierce perfectionist who never accepted weakness in any area of his game, relentlessly practising until he felt confident in every department. 'If you want to increase your success rate,' he once said, 'double your failure rate.'

Mavericks

Not every golfer is remembered for the number of Majors he won. Some are fondly recalled for their character, their temperament or even for what they wore. Here's a few of the game's most notorious mavericks.

John Daly

Hard-drinking, heavy-smoking Southern boy John Daly burst onto the scene in 1991 with a PGA Championship victory that came right out of the blue. Daly wasn't even supposed to compete in the event, qualifying as the ninth alternate choice when Nick Price dropped out at the last moment. Without even enjoying the benefit of a practice round, he stormed the tournament by three strokes, thanks mainly to his superhuman driving. A further Major came in 1995 when he won The Open, but by then the cracks were already beginning to appear. Daly endured something of a royal flush of personal problems. An alcoholic and a constant smoker, he gambled away most of his winnings and expanded to a weight of nearly 300lbs before going through three divorces, gastric surgery and, rather unsurprisingly, mental exhaustion. A comeback in 2008 gave his legions of fans new hope, but the news that he had been taken into protective custody outside a Hooters restaurant later in the same year gave the golfing world the distinct impression that Daly's best years had long since passed him by.

Payne Stewart

Missouri-born Payne Stewart was a huge fans' favourite in the 1990s, partly because of the talent that led him to three Major wins, but mainly for his eccentric dress sense. You remember those silly trousers we discussed in the introduction? Well, Stewart absolutely adored them. He was reputed to have the largest wardrobe on the circuit, filled with the kind of things that, if your dad wore them, would make you crumple in humiliation. Somehow though, Stewart could pull it off. Knickerbockers and floppy hats? He could do it. Plus fours and a tam-o'-shanter? He did it. Tragically, his life was cut short just months after winning his second US Open in 1999. Travelling in a Learjet to the final tournament of the PGA season, a sudden loss of cabin pressure incapacitated everyone aboard in a matter of moments. Unable to raise the pilots on the radio, military jets flanked the doomed plane until it ran out of fuel and crashed into a field in South Dakota.

Ian Poulter

The natural heir to Stewart's throne, Ian Poulter is the UK's most ebullient and eccentric golfer, as well as being a fine player in his own right. Famous for the Union Jack slacks that he wore in the 2004 Ryder Cup, he has cultivated something of a reputation as a wild child, an unfair jibe given that he is happily married with three children. Poulter may not have the natural class of Stewart, as shown when he wore an Arsenal football shirt during an event, but he does keep the place looking bright and cheerful. That said, he also has a bit of a temper on him. Fined in 2006 for verbally abusing a marshal, he threw a huge wobbly in 2009 when a photographer took a loud snap of him on his backswing. Poulter was not amused and enjoyed what politicians refer to as a 'full and frank exchange of views' with the hapless snapper.

Greatest mistakes

There isn't a player alive who has never made a mistake. Everyone has had that moment when the green seems easily reachable with a pitching wedge, or when the green keepers have filled the bunkers with golf ball magnets. You can play a fine round of golf for 17 holes, but it only takes one shank on the 18th to ruin everything. Rest assured though, whatever you've done wrong, wherever you've failed, someone else has done it worse and on a far bigger stage. Here's a few of the most infamous bloopers.

Jean Van de Velde

In an alternative universe, doing a 'Van de Velde' means to overturn fearsome odds and succeed. In a parallel dimension out there somewhere, the Frenchman must make a fortune on the after-dinner speaking circuit, picking out lines from a series of best-selling self-help books. Something of a shame then that, in this world, his name is a byword for failure, synonymous with the act of snatching defeat from the jaws of victory.

Jean Van de Velde was a relatively unheralded golfer, but he had the weekend of his life at Carnoustie in 1999 while playing for The Open. Leading by several shots as he approached the 18th hole on the final day, he could have shot a double bogey, a six on this par 4, and still lifted the Claret Jug. All he had to do was just hold his nerve and play it safe. Fat chance.

His emphatic drive stopped in the rough, perilously short of a stream and, instead of playing safe and laying up, he decided to hammer the second one towards the green. It ended up in jungle. From there, he shot for the green again, landing the ball straight in another stream. So desperate was he not to drop a penalty stroke, he even took his shoes and socks off and considered playing the ball out of the water, an act of such extraordinary foolishness that BBC commentator Peter Alliss was publicly begging someone to run down and stop him. Mercifully, he opted against an aquatic attempt and decided to take the penalty, but the next shot ended up in the bunker. He eventually holed on his seventh shot, a triple bogey that forced a play-off for the title. Unsurprisingly, with his nerves shot to pieces, Van de Velde lost and The Open was won by Paul Lawrie instead.

Colin Montgomerie

Poor Colin Montgomerie is the nearly man of international golf. He's been a legend on the European Tour and a stalwart of the Ryder Cup team, but he's never managed to win a Major and he'll never come closer than he did in the 2006 US Open.

After an astonishing 45-yard birdie on the 17th, he was tied for the lead on the final hole of the final day. All he needed to do was land a shot on the green and tuck the ball up for the title, but it all went wrong because of one silly decision. For some reason, the irascible Scotsman decided to switch from a

6 Iron to a 7 Iron, reducing the distance of his shot. Instead of bouncing happily onto the green, the ball fell short, the follow-up went all the way to the back of the green and, when Monty missed his long putt, it was Australia's Geoff Ogilvy who went on to win the tournament.

Miles Byrne

A caddy doesn't have many jobs. Primarily, he must carry the bag and it's nice if he can offer some good advice along the way. Aside from that, he needs only a chirpy nature and the ability to carry out basic administration. It was the latter that did for the wretched Miles Byrne.

There is a rule, explained earlier in these pages, about the number of clubs a golfer can have in his bag. Any more than 14 and you're breaking the rules. Byrne, caddying for the Welsh golfer Ian Woosnam, forgot about all this and let his boss wander out onto the final round of The Open in 2000 with 15 clubs. Realising that something didn't add up at the second hole, Woosnam incurred a critical two-stroke penalty. Furious at Byrne, he threw the extra club away in disgust, stormed around the next few holes and eventually regained his composure only to lose out on the Jug by three shots.

Astonishingly, rather than kicking him up and down the Royal Lytham golf course, Woosnam publicly forgave his caddy for his mistake.

'He commited the ultimate sin and he will not do it again,' said Woosnam. 'It's the biggest mistake that he will ever make and he will have a severe rollicking, but he's a good lad and I'm not going to sack him.'

Unfortunately, Woosnam was wrong. It wasn't the biggest mistake that Byrne would ever make and it would take less than a fortnight for him to best it. With his boss in action in Malmo for the Scandinavian Masters, Byrne overslept and missed the 7.15am tee-off. Woosnam was forced to break into his own locker to retrieve his golf shoes and, as there were no extra caddies available, had to take the local caddy-master with him instead. Poor Tommy Strand only had three minutes' notice before his call to action and Byrne, when he eventually materialised, was sacked on the spot to the surprise of absolutely nobody.

Taking up golf

Mention out loud that you're considering taking up golf and you might be lucky enough to hear a cry of 'NOOOO! SAVE YOURSELF!' from all manner of well-meaning friends and relatives. Golf is a wonderful game, but it will cost you thousands of pounds, thousands of hours and possibly your sanity. That said, it's also good exercise, good fun and a nice break from the daily grind. Some people also claim that it relieves stress, but – judging from my own inept and infuriating performances – I'm not so sure about that.

There are hundreds of instructional books on golf available in the shops, but it'd probably be best to get some proper lessons before you do anything else. Check your local phone directory: you'll have a local golf club and they will almost certainly have a resident professional. Failing that, there are always freelance instructors available. It's best to have someone who knows what they're talking about to teach you from the start, otherwise you could find yourself picking up all kinds of nasty habits that take years to eradicate from your game.

You'll also want to find yourself a local driving range. Driving ranges are excellent places to practise your swing, or try out a new club. You can wander along with your golf bag, find a spot in the shooting gallery and blast away to your heart's content. Most ranges charge only by the number of balls that you use, usually employing a machine to dispense them into a bucket. They're a cheap and easy way to improve your skills.

Less cheap, but much more fun, are the golf simulators that I alluded to earlier in this book. Urban Golf, to name one of them, is an indoor golf course made up, in true *Matrix*-style, of small virtual reality booths with a huge projection screen at one end showing your position on a golf course. Wallop a ball at the screen and it passes through dozens of tiny laser beams that measure its progress, speed, direction and spin. By the time the physical ball hits the screen and drops to the floor, a small computer-generated ball appears and takes its place, continuing the journey in pixel form. This version of the game has a number of advantages, namely that you can enjoy beer and sandwiches during the game and that you don't have to yomp over 6 miles of countryside while you do it.

Finally, there is the oft-mocked format of crazy golf, which remains a fantastic way to improve your putting game. After all, if you can tap a ball across a drawbridge, round a helter-skelter and down a slope between two large fibreglass soldiers into the hole, what possible fear could a tricky slope on the 16th green induce? It's cheap, it's fun and you can pretend that you're playing it simply to keep the kids amused, when all the while you're doing it to improve your putting game.

Golf, as has already been mentioned, is a fine game, a passport to new friendships and the key to a wider understanding of that eternal battle between ambition and patience. It is, however, incredibly frustrating and unforgiving. There are many ways to learn, even more methods for improvement and you'll never be short of potential advisors, but it will never ever become an 'easy' game. Make sure you understand that before you pick up your first club...

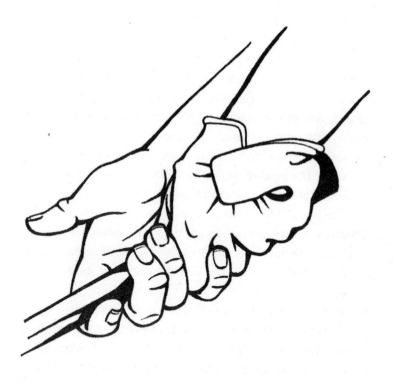

Glossary

Address   The warm-up where a golfer will gently approach the ball with his club before ripping back and hitting it for real. Be careful though, if you accidentally move the ball then a penalty stroke is invoked.

Air-shot   The kind of thing that I do – swinging and missing the ball. It's really quite embarrassing.

Albatross   Three shots under par on a hole, otherwise known as a double eagle. It's an almost unbelievable achievement requiring two absolutely enormous and incredibly accurate shots.

Approach   The shot that takes the player to the green. On a par 4, you'd tee off and then look to approach the green on the second shot. Then, depending on how close you get to the hole, you've got one putt to get close and one to get down. A great approach shot therefore would be one that didn't just reach the green, but that got close to the hole as well, giving the player a chance of a birdie. Good approach play is vital for any top player.

Augusta The home of the US Masters, a gorgeous golf course in the heart of Georgia, USA. Scene of Tiger Woods' astonishing 12-stroke victory in 1997.

Backswing The part of the swing where the club is behind you. Never speak during another man's backswing and never get in the way of one – it's just not the done thing.

Bag The large fabric container used to carry clubs, balls, tees, scorecards, hip flasks, cigars and all the other assorted paraphernalia of your average golfer.

Ball You can't play golf without a golf ball. Small and white and usually marked with a brand logo, it's covered in dimples to help it fly further and truer. Try to avoid being hit by one because it really, really hurts.

Belly putter An extended version of the standard putter, designed to rest against the abdomen of the player, increasing stability and lessening the reliance on the wrists, the source of nearly all misplaced putts.

Birdie To complete a hole one shot under the par. A three on a par 4, if you will. Everyone likes a birdie.

Bogey To complete a hole one shot over the par. No one wants a bogey.

Broomstick putter A very long putter, about the length of a broomstick oddly enough, that minimises the chance of a loose wrist ruining a putt shot. Not many people use these long putters because what they give in control they take away in feeling. They can, however, be very effective tools for a player who suffers from the yips.

Bunker A large hole filled with sand, usually positioned right under the flight path of your ball. Bunkers are the creation of the Devil himself, as anyone who has ever been trapped in one will testify. The sand swallows up the ball, you see, making it far more difficult to hit. Some bunkers are benign affairs, shaped like long-jump pits, but others are far more evil. There are some bunkers out there so deep that you can't actually see out of them.

Caddies The men and women who carry the bags, fill out the scorecards, count the clubs and dish out bits of advice like, 'Don't hit the ball towards that big sandpit.' A good caddy can save a bad golfer from himself; a bad one is just a porter with a pencil.

Chip A gentle little shot used to lift the ball up onto the green from close range. You can practise a chip shot in your back garden with a pitching wedge and an upturned bucket. There you go! And I said there wouldn't be any coaching tips in here…

Claret Jug The reward for the winner of The Open. Remember, that's The Open, not the British Open, UK Open or any other kind of Open. Just The Open.

Club The big stick used to hit the ball. Clubs come in all shapes and sizes and are chosen specifically for their range and for the angle of their face. A lofted club will hit a ball high and short, a flatter one will hit it further.

Concede Used in match play when one hapless player acknowledges that he's never, ever going to win the hole and that he would save everyone an awful lot of time by just giving up and moving onto the next one.

Condor Four shots under par on a hole or, in other words, a hole in one on a par 5. This almost never happens and is thought by some to be a myth, like the Loch Ness Monster, Bigfoot and a completely original song by Oasis.

Course The golf course, of course.

Course management Basically a way of describing someone's ability to use tactics. If you keep laying up and avoiding hazards while all about you go splashing around in the drink, then your course management is obviously very impressive. It's also a way of recognising the ability of a player to know what's coming, to aim for the most advantageous part of the fairway, or to land on the area of the green that poses the least amount of problems.

Crazy golf A magnificent take on the putting game where the full-sized golf course is replaced by a novelty themed, small-scale obstacle course generally made up of bridges, tunnels, fibre-glass castles and, at the magnificent crazy golf course in South Shields, England, pirate-themed 'har-hargh!'-type shenanigans.

Cut The method used to thin out the pack in the second half of a competition. After two rounds, only the players within ten shots of the leader are allowed to continue. The others will 'miss the cut'.

Dance floor   A slang name for the green.

Divot   A large lump of grass and earth ripped out of the golf course by a poor shot. Divots must always be replaced back in the ground before the greenkeeper finds out what you've done or someone else's ball gets stuck in them.

Dogleg   A hole with a visible, but gradual, corner somewhere in the middle. Unless you're a master of the draw/fade, then you'll need one shot to get to the corner of the dogleg and then another to advance towards the hole. Or you can just try and spank it over the trees that guard the corner itself. Be wary though … they've been planted there for a reason.

Draw   The opposite of the 'fade', the draw is a specialised golf shot that, for a right-handed player, sends the ball gently from the right to the left in mid-air. A left-handed player would draw the ball from left to right. A good draw can send a ball round a dogleg like a chauffeur-driven limousine. If you 'draw' the ball without meaning to, it's actually a hook. Nowhere near as good.

Dress code   Many golf clubs have a dress code that you'll need to adhere to before they let you in the front door. Always check before turning up in a cowboy hat and a sequinned denim jacket.

Drink   A slang term for a water hazard. No one wants to send the ball in the drink, there's a one-stroke penalty for that kind of offence.

Drive   A powerful shot from the tee.

Driver   The big-headed monster of a club used to absolutely spank the ball down the fairway from tee. It can also be used on the fairway itself, but it requires great expertise.

Eagle   Two shots under par on a hole. A fantastic achievement.

European Order of Merit   The former moniker for what is now the Race to Dubai. Essentially, this is the European PGA Tour by a different name.

Fade   The opposite of the 'draw', the fade is a specialised golf shot that, for a right-handed player, sends the ball gently from left to right in mid-air. A left-handed player would fade the ball from right to left. Fades and draws are only executable by advanced players, but they can prove to be absolutely invaluable for dealing with difficult courses.

Fairway   The shortish grass that marks the way to the green. A ball on the fairway is nice and easy to hit. A ball in the rough to either side of it is most certainly not. The simple objective of every golfer at the tee-shot is to hit the fairway. Everything else will follow in time.

Flag   The flag marks the position of the hole. If in doubt, aim for it.

Flop   A specialised golf shot executable only with an open-faced club, like a pitching or sand wedge for example. A flop shot sends the ball up in the air and back down again without travelling too far. It's a good way of getting over obstacles without sending the ball rolling miles past your target.

Fore The traditional shout of the concerned golfer. If your ball is heading out of sight or, worse still, towards a group of people, you are obliged to bellow 'Fore!' at the top of your voice. This comes from the days when rich golfers would have two caddies, one to hold the bag and one brave soul to walk out ahead and be there to spot where the ball landed. Golfers would shout 'Forecaddy!' before eventually realising that in the time it took to get three syllables out at volume, the poor fellow was probably already dead.

Fourball A four-player game with two teams of two. Each player has his own ball but only the lowest score of each pair is entered on the scorecard.

Foursome A four-player game with two teams of two. Each player plays the alternate shot to his partner.

Fried egg A ball that lands in the sand and almost disappears from view. Fried eggs are really difficult to hit, so bring your sand wedge and an infinite amount of patience.

Fringe The very edge of the green, with slightly rougher grass than you'd find in the centre. You can still putt from here, but it's not going to be easy.

Grand Slam The name given to the achievement of winning all four Majors in the same season. Well, I say 'achievement', but no one's actually ever managed it. Ben Hogan and Tiger Woods have come close, but it remains the Holy Grail of the sport.

Green The immaculately coiffured area of grass surrounding the flagpole and the hole. Once you're on the green, you can whip out the putter and start trying to sink the ball in the hole. Greenkeepers spend most of their lives attending to the greens, flattening and trimming them, coaxing them towards perfection. If they find you messing them up, they'll actually kill you, like, really dead.

Green in Regulation (GIR) If you can get to the green, leaving yourself with two shots to make par, then you've achieved a GIR. Reaching the green of a par 5 on three shots would be sufficient, as would the green of a par 4 on two.

Grounding the club Pushing the head of the club into the ground to diminish the threat caused by a hazard. Grounding the club in sand would be a good way of curing a 'fried egg' (see above) if it wasn't completely against the rules.

Hacking Moving around the course with very little style or finesse, impatiently and amateurishly swinging at the ball without success. A hack is the derogatory name given to a poor player. A poor player who, like me, was also a journalist would, therefore, be a hackhack. Or a hack squared. I'm not really sure to be honest with you.

Halved To share a hole in match play, scoring the same and tying the hole.

Handicap The method used to allow players of different abilities to play together. In its most basic form, if I could generally get myself around a golf course using fifteen more shots than par, and you could do it with just five more than par, then you would be a better player than me by a margin of ten shots. If we played together, you would almost always win and that would be no fun for me. However, if we used the handicap system, then I would get a ten-shot head start and it would be far more interesting. We could even put money on it. Come on, let's put money on it. What are you? Chicken?

Hazards The nasty things that course designers include to ruin your day. Bunkers, deep and shallow, are a right royal pain in the backside, but water hazards are the real nightmare. Bunkers will only slow you down, but water will cost you a penalty stroke.

Hole Ah, the glorious endgame. There is only one objective in golf: get the ball in the hole. The hole is always 4.25 inches in diameter. This is because of the good people at the Royal and Ancient Golf Club of St Andrews who invented the first golf hole cutter in 1829, a device used for removing a perfect tube of earth from the ground. The cutter had a diameter of 4.25 inches. You can still see the old cutter in a museum, you know, if you like that kind of thing...

Hole in one Hitting the ball from the tee to the hole, a truly magical moment in any golfer's life, but one that will cost him an awful lot in drinks. Also known by our American cousins as an 'ace'.

Hook A shot that starts right and then veers left as if it's spotted something in the rough that it really, really likes. A draw shot is a deliberate right-to-left deviation; a hook moves in the same direction, but without you actually meaning to do it.

Hosel The part of the club between the club head and the shaft. Hit the ball with the hosel and you'll have what is commonly known as a 'shank', where the ball clatters off as if you've hit it with a mallet.

Iron The steel-shafted clubs that run from a 1 Iron to a 9 Iron, used for hitting the ball short to medium-long distances.

The Ladies Professional Golf Association (LPGA) The organisational body that runs the women's game.

Lay up A conservative tactic used to minimise the chance of humiliation. If you're hitting down a fairway and there's a stream cutting across in front of you, you might want to think about laying up and deliberately playing the ball shorter than you know you can hit it. A braver, or stupider, player would sneer at this and just hit it as hard as he could, hoping against hope to clear the hazard. Sometimes it will work and he'll gain the advantage. Sometimes it won't and the meek will inherit the hole.

Leaderboard The big board on display at golf competitions with the scores on. If you're top of the leaderboard, then you're on your way to a trophy of some kind. Unless it all goes horribly wrong of course...

Lie The position of the ball after you've hit it. A good lie would be on the fairway, a favourable lie might be if it landed on top of some fairly short rough, or on the sand without burying itself. A bad lie would be behind a tree, or buried deep in the bunker.

Links   An old fashioned course marked out on coastal land, like St Andrews.

Lip   The rim of the hole. If the ball rolls over this it will either begin a gentle circle and then drop in or it will whizz round and shoot off into the distance.

Masters   One of the four Majors, but the only one to be held at the same venue, Augusta, every year.

Match play   The form of golf where every hole is an individual competition. You can have an absolute nightmare on the first hole, but it will bear no relevance to your eventual score. You could take 15 strokes on a par 3, but you'd still only lose the hole. By the second hole, you'd simply be one down and you could draw level if you won by just one stroke.

Major   One of the four big golf tournaments, either The Open, the US Open, the Masters or the PGA Championship.

Mulligan   Some very casual players have an unofficial rule allowing players a certain number of Mulligans every round. This enables a player to simply ignore a really disastrous shot and play it again as if it never happened. You won't see any Mulligans in competitions. There are a number of explanations for the origin of the phrase, none of which have any hard evidence to back them up. The most common theory is that it was based on the incompetence of a prominent North American club player of the 1920s, either a David Mulligan or a John 'Buddy' Mulligan, depending on who you believe. There is also a theory that it was a sniffy reaction to the large numbers of Irish-Americans joining US golf clubs in the 20th century and the apparent lack of success of their efforts.

Nerve Golf is all about holding your nerve, keeping your cool, maintaining your composure. It's an invisible commodity, but no less valuable for that.

Open A competition that, technically, is open to anyone. Obviously, you have to be a very good golfer to qualify, though. You can't just turn up with your clubs and get a game with Tiger Woods.

Out of bounds A shot that is so bad that it leaves the boundaries of the hole itself, sometimes landing on an entirely different hole instead. This is the kind of incompetence that leads to a one-stroke penalty and the unbridled mirth of your companions.

Par The number of shots that a hole or a course should be completed in. A par 4 is a hole that should require four shots. A golfer who finishes a 72-shot round two over par will have gone round in 74.

Penalty A penalty stroke can be added to the scorecard in the event of an infraction of the rules. For example, if you were to hit the ball in the water on your first shot, you would incur a one-stroke penalty. Your next shot would be your third.

PGA Championship The final Major in the golfing season, occasionally known for this reason as 'glory's last shot'.

PGA Tour The biggest professional golf tour in the world.

Pin The pin is the affectionate nickname given to the flagpole.

Pitch A pitched shot is designed to go high and not particularly far, usually to travel from the end of the fairway to the green, a distance of around 50 yards or so.

Pro-Am Simply, 'Professional–amateur'. A tournament that has a mix of the two levels, something which is easy enough to arrange thanks to the handicap system, or the team-based meritocracy of the fourball format. Many Pro-Am tournaments include a number of famous players to give the status 'Celebrity Pro-Am'.

The Professional Golfers' Association of America (PGA) One of the largest sports organisations in the world, dedicated to furthering the enjoyment of the game.

Punch If you're trapped under the branches of trees or playing in windy conditions, a punch shot is used to make the ball travel a long distance but at a relatively low altitude.

Putt To hit the ball on the green into the hole with your putter. A successful shot from outside the green, say with a wedge from 50 yards, is not a putt. It is incredibly impressive and something to tell your friends about, but it's not a putt. Incidentally, you should know that you pronounce 'putt' to rhyme with 'shut' and not to rhyme with foot. It's a putting game, not a pooting game, if you know what I mean.

Putter The club specifically designed to putt the ball.

Putting game The ability of a player to putt. If your putting game goes to pieces then you'll find it very difficult to ever win a game of golf again. A good putting game, by contrast, will hide a multitude of errors.

Putting line The imaginary line that links the position of the ball on the green to the hole. If the line crosses slopes or imperfections, then the golfer must adapt his shot to compensate. If someone walks across the line, scuffing the grass or leaving a mark from their spiky shoes, the golfer must attack and immobilise that person as a warning to others. Possibly.

Rookie The name given to a player in his first season on a professional tour. The PGA Tour has a Rookie of the Year Award given to the most impressive newcomer.

Rough The haggard, long grass outside of the fairway. Put a ball here and it's much, much more difficult to hit. Depending on the length of the grass, rough can be anything from a mild inconvenience to a round-ruining disaster.

Round The full 18 holes of a golf course. You can play the front nine, the back nine or the full round.

Royal and Ancient Golf Club The golf club at St Andrews, an influential body who co-manage the rules of golf along with the USGA (see below).

Ryder Cup   The prestigious match play competition between the USA and Europe, held every two years. The two 12-man teams go at it hammer and tongs over three days of head-to-head competition. It's really very exciting.

St Andrews   The home of golf, a historic links course in Scotland. St Andrews hosts The Open approximately every five years. The weather is usually abysmal.

Scorecard   The little piece of paper with all of your scores on. Keep it safe and try not to make any mistakes. A bad scorecard would be one with lots of high numbers on it.

Scratch   The name given to a player whose handicap drops down to zero, essentially making him the same standard as a professional player.

Shank   The horrible moment when the wrong bit of the club makes contact with the ball and it veers off in the wrong direction making a horrible noise as it goes. Only the clubface should ever hit the ball, not the hosel, which is the bit that holds it to the shaft. Everyone shanks from time to time, but that doesn't make it any easier to bear.

Short game   A generic phrase used to describe short-range approach shots. If you take the tee-shot as the first stage of the game and the putt as the end stage, then the short game is usually the bit in between where a player tries to travel from the fairway to the green. You might be able use a good drive to get you further off the tee than your friends, but without a good short game, it's worth absolutely nothing. You can save yourself shots with a short game, but you can only save yourself a handful of yards with a good drive.

Signature hole The most famous, notorious or recognisable hole on a golf course. Not strictly an official term, but one that is used regularly regardless.

Skins A form of match play golf where every hole is worth a certain amount of money. Win the hole, win the money. Draw the hole and the money rolls over to the next one. The player with the most money at the end is the winner.

Slice If your golf ball veers from left to right after being hit then the chances are that you've developed a slice. You need to get yourself to a driving range and practise until you get rid of it.

Slacks Casual trousers. Not jeans, not shorts, just good, sturdy sensible slacks. Great Britain was built by men who wore slacks.

Solheim Cup The women's version of the Ryder Cup, played in an identical style.

Stableford A slightly complicated points-scoring system of golf. Points are awarded at every hole for performance, with more on offer for birdies than bogeys and so on. Stableford used to be quite popular, but its appeal has waned in recent years.

Stroke A shot, basically, but a much smoother way of saying it. Golfers will want to get round a par 4 in four strokes.

Stroke play The form of golf where the winner is determined by the number of strokes made. Go round the 18 holes in 72 and you'll beat someone who went round in 73. It's a far more balanced and telling test of your golfing abilities, mainly because one mistake can cost you the entire afternoon. It's a cruel game.

Swing The act of bringing the club back behind your head and then whooshing it down upon the ball.

Tee The little plastic object that you put the ball on before you hit it. You can only use a tee on your first shot, hence the term 'teeing off'.

Tee-shot The first shot of the hole, where the golfer blasts the ball off the tee and, hopefully, straight down the fairway.

Thwock The utterly gorgeous noise you hear when you hit the ball just right. The first time you hear it is like your first kiss, but much better and with less tongue.

Tiger-proofing The phenomenon of golf clubs anxiously changing the lengths of their fairways and the size of their greens in an effort to stop Tiger Woods from winning all the time. Mind you, it didn't work very well. Lengthening the course just made it even more difficult for anyone to compete with Woods' power. If they'd thought about it, maybe they'd have shortened everything instead.

Tour Golfers sign up to play on tours which last the entire year and travel to different regions of the world. The best tour to be on is the PGA Tour, but there is also the European Tour, as well as a number of senior and amateur tours.

The United States Golf Association (USGA) The governing body of golf in the USA and Mexico.

Urban Golf The excellent hi-tech golf simulator where you can practise indoors by hitting balls through incredibly clever laser beams while your performance is replicated on screen in computer graphics. Basically, it's golf without the walking and you can get people to bring you beer and sandwiches.

Wedge Wedges are open-faced clubs designed for lifting the ball high into the air. A pitching wedge is something of an all-purpose affair, but sand wedges are particularly good in bunkers.

Wood A wooden-headed club used for striking the ball enormous distances.

Yips The nervous condition that makes golfers twitch or flinch when they take important shots. It could be a mental condition, it could be a muscular problem, but in either case it's a very good way of ruining a promising career in professional golf.

Index

Also available:

Everything You Ever Wanted to Know About Rugby But Were too Afraid to Ask

ISBN: 9781408114940

Everything You Ever Wanted to Know About Cricket But Were too Afraid to Ask

ISBN: 9781408114957

Everything You Ever Wanted to Know About Football But Were too Afraid to Ask

ISBN: 9781408114964